KT-453-205

The Dorling Kindersley

ILLUSTRATED FAMILY ENCYCLOPEDIA

VOLUME 1 CONTENTS, A – ARCTIC

DK

LONDON, NEW YORK, MUNICH, MELBOURNE AND DELHI

Senior Editor Jayne Parsons   **Senior Art Editor** Gillian Shaw

Project Editors
Marian Broderick, Gill Cooling,
Maggie Crowley, Hazel Egerton,
Cynthia O'Neill, Veronica Pennycook,
Louise Pritchard, Steve Setford, Jackie Wilson

Project Art Editors
Jane Felstead, Martyn Foote,
Neville Graham, Jamie Hanson,
Christopher Howson, Jill Plank, Floyd Sayers,
Jane Tetzlaff, Ann Thompson

Editors
Rachel Beaugié, Nic Kynaston, Sarah Levete,
Karen O'Brien, Linda Sonntag

Art Editors
Tina Borg, Diane Clouting,
Tory Gordon-Harris

DTP Designers
Andrew O'Brien, Cordelia Springer

Managing Editor Ann Kramer   **Managing Art Editor** Peter Bailey

Senior DTP Designer Mathew Birch

Picture Research Jo Walton, Kate Duncan, Liz Moore

DK Picture Library Ola Rudowska, Melanie Simmonds

Country pages by PAGE*One*: Bob Gordon, Helen Parker,
Thomas Keenes, Sarah Watson, Chris Clark

Cartographers Peter Winfield, James Anderson

Research Robert Graham, Angela Koo

Editorial Assistants Sarah-Louise Reed, Nichola Roberts

Production Louise Barratt, Charlotte Traill

First published in Great Britain in 1997, 2004
by Dorling Kindersley Limited,
80 Strand, London WC2R 0RL

Copyright © 1997, © 2004 Dorling Kindersley Limited, London
A Penguin company

This edition published in 2004 by MDS BOOKS/MEDIASAT Group in association with MediaFund Limited

www.mediasatgroup.com

All rights reserved. No part of this publication may be reproduced, stored in a
retrieval system, or transmitted by any means, electronic, photocopying, recording,
or otherwise, without the prior permission of the copyright owner.

A CIP catalogue record for this book is available from the British Library

ISBN: 84 9789 537 1 (ISBN of the collection)
ISBN: 84 9789 520 7 (ISBN of this volume)
ISSN: 1744 2214

Not to be sold separately from the Daily Mail

Colour reproduction by Colourscan, Singapore
Printed and bound in the E.U.

LIST OF MAIN ENTRIES, VOLUMES 1–16

See index for further topics

POWER AND SPEED

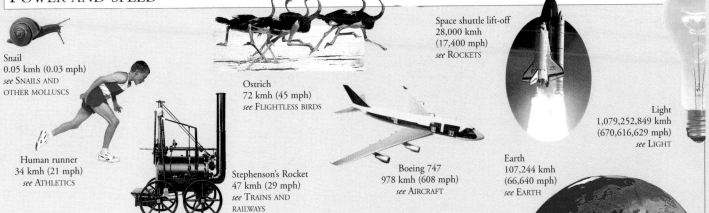

Snail
0.05 kmh (0.03 mph)
see Snails and
other molluscs

Human runner
34 kmh (21 mph)
see Athletics

Stephenson's Rocket
47 kmh (29 mph)
see Trains and
railways

Ostrich
72 kmh (45 mph)
see Flightless birds

Boeing 747
978 kmh (608 mph)
see Aircraft

Space shuttle lift-off
28,000 kmh
(17,400 mph)
see Rockets

Earth
107,244 kmh
(66,640 mph)
see Earth

Light
1,079,252,849 kmh
(670,616,629 mph)
see Light

Jupiter, the largest planet,
comparative to the Sun

Sun see SUN AND SOLAR SYSTEM

COMPARATIVE PLANET SIZES

Uranus *see* PLANETS

Neptune *see* PLANETS

Pluto
see PLANETS

Mars
see PLANETS

Earth
see EARTH

Mercury
see PLANETS

Venus
see PLANETS

Saturn
see PLANETS

Jupiter
see PLANETS

COMMUNICATION TIMELINE

490 BC
Marathon runner
see OLYMPIC
GAMES

Carrier pigeon
see BIRDS

18th century Sign language
see LANGUAGES

1840
Postage stamp
see STAMPS AND
POSTAL SERVICES

1837
Electric
telegraph
see TELECOMMUNICATIONS

1844
Morse code
see CODES AND
CIPHERS

1876
Bell telephone
see TELEPHONES

| 12th century Smoke signals | 1784 Mail coach | 1850 Pillar box | 1855 Printing telegraph | 1860 Semaphore and Pony Express | 1861 Postcards |

1889 Coin-operated telephone *see* TELEPHONES

1896 Radio transmitter *see* RADIO

1926 Baird television *see* INVENTIONS

1933–35 Radar *see* RADAR AND SONAR

1983 Satellite television *see* SATELLITES

1980s–90s Mobile telephone *see* TELEPHONES

1990s Videophone *see* TELEPHONES

1891 Dial telephones   1919 Airmail   1954 Transistor radio   1962 Communications satellite   1964 Word processor   1980s Fax machine

HOW TO USE THIS ENCYCLOPEDIA

THE FOLLOWING PAGES WILL HELP YOU get the most out of your copy of the *Dorling Kindersley Illustrated Family Encyclopedia*. The encyclopedia consists of three volumes. Volumes 1–2 contain nearly 700 main entries organized alphabetically, from Aboriginal Australians through to Zoos. To find the entry you want, simply turn to the correct letter of the alphabet.

If you cannot find the topic you want, then turn to Volume 3. This volume includes an index and gazetteer for the whole encyclopedia, which will direct you straight to the page you need. In addition, Volume 3 contains hundreds of reference charts, fact boxes, lists, and tables to supplement the information provided on the main entry pages.

MEASUREMENTS AND ABBREVIATIONS

Most measurements are supplied in both metric and imperial units. Some of the most common abbreviations used in the encyclopedia are shown below in **bold** type.

°C = degrees Celsius
°F = degrees Fahrenheit
K = degrees kelvin
mm = millimetre; **cm** = centimetre
m = metre; **km** = kilometre
in = inch; **ft** = foot; **yd** = yard
g = gram; **kg** = kilogram
oz = ounce; **lb** = pound
ml = millilitre; **l** = litre
pt = pint; **gal** = gallon
sq km (km²) = square kilometre
sq ft (ft²) = square foot
kmh = kilometres per hour
mph = miles per hour
mya = million years ago
BC = before Christ
AD = anno Domini (refers to any date after the birth of Christ)
c. = circa (about)
b. = born; **d.** = died; **r.** = reigned

THE PAGE LAYOUT

The pages in this encyclopedia have been carefully planned to make each subject as accessible as possible. Main entries are broken down into a hierarchy of information – from a general introduction to more specific individual topics.

Alphabet locators

Letter flashes help you find your way quickly around the encyclopedia.

Sub-entries

Sub-entries provide important additional information and expand on points made in the introduction.

This sub-entry explains how rainbows are caused by raindrops in the air.

Diagrams

Clear diagrams help explain complex processes and scientific concepts.

The diagram here shows how a raindrop splits sunlight into its constituent colours.

Introduction

Clear introductions are the starting point for each entry. The introduction defines and provides an overview of each subject.

In the main entry on COLOUR, the introduction explains that colours are different forms of light, and that sunlight contains light of many different colours.

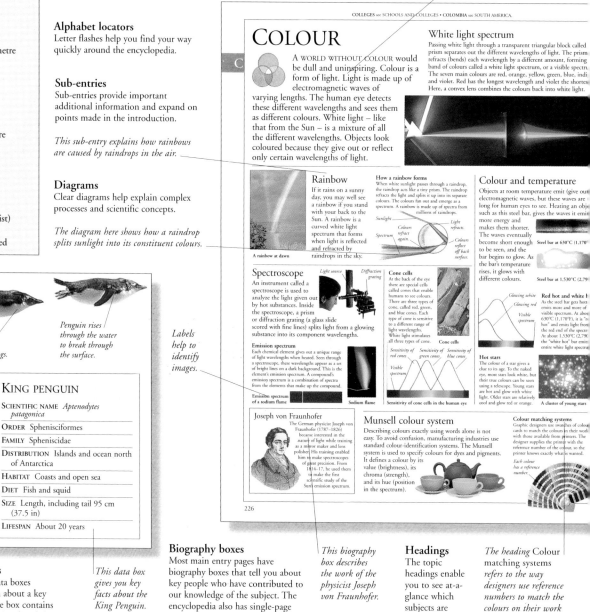

Labels help to identify images.

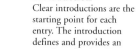

Strong chest muscles pull down the wings.

act as rudders.

Penguin rises through the water to break through the surface.

Huddling reduces heat loss.

emperor penguins carry chicks around on their feet.

KING PENGUIN

SCIENTIFIC NAME *Aptenodytes patagonica*

ORDER Sphenisciformes

FAMILY Spheniscidae

DISTRIBUTION Islands and ocean north of Antarctica

HABITAT Coasts and open sea

DIET Fish and squid

SIZE Length, including tail 95 cm (37.5 in)

LIFESPAN About 20 years

Natural history data boxes

On the natural history pages, data boxes summarize essential information about a key animal featured in the entry. The box contains information about the animal's size, diet, habitat, lifespan, distribution, and scientific name.

This data box gives you key facts about the King Penguin.

Biography boxes

Most main entry pages have biography boxes that tell you about key people who have contributed to our knowledge of the subject. The encyclopedia also has single-page entries on the life and work of more than 50 major historical figures.

This biography box describes the work of the physicist Joseph von Fraunhofer.

Headings

The topic headings enable you to see at-a-glance which subjects are covered within the main entry.

The heading Colour matching systems refers to the way designers use reference numbers to match the colours on their work to the colours of printers' inks.

INDEX

Volume 3 contains an index and a gazetteer. The index, which comes first, lists all the topics mentioned in the encyclopedia and the pages on which they can be found. The gazetteer follows on, with references to help you find all the features included on the maps.

- page numbers in **bold** type (eg Knights and heraldry **495-6**) show that the subject is a main A–Z entry in Volumes 1–2.
- page numbers in plain type (eg armour 69) send you to sub-entries, text references, and the reference section.
- grid references (eg Cremona Italy 475 C3) are letter-number combinations that locate features on maps.

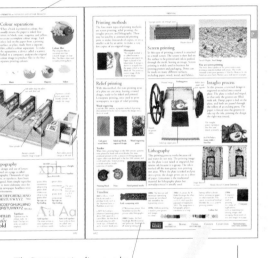

This two-page entry discusses the main types of primate.

Running head

There is an A–Z running head at the top of most pages to help you find important topics that are not main entries within the encyclopedia.

The running head on PRINTING tells you that although there is no main entry on primates, you can find the topic on MONKEYS AND OTHER PRIMATES.

Illustrations

Each main entry is heavily illustrated with models, photographs, and artworks, adding a vibrant layer of visual information to the page.

This annotation tells you how different colours can be produced by mixing red, green, and blue light.

Annotation

The illustrations are comprehensively annotated to draw attention to details of particular interest and to explain complex points.

Picture is made up of tiny ink dots.

Timelines

An entry may include a timeline that gives the dates of key events in the history or development of the subject.

The PRINTING timeline stretches from the printing of the first books in ancient China to the computerization of modern printing.

COLLECTION PAGES

There are more than 70 pages of photographic collections, which follow main entries and provide a visual guide to the subject. They are organized under clear headings.

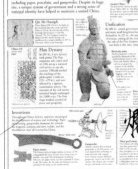

Find out more

The Find Out More lines at the end of each entry direct you to other relevant main entries in the encyclopedia. Using the Find Out More lines can help you understand an entry in its wider context.

On COLOUR, the Find Out More line directs you to the entry on PRINTING, where there is a detailed explanation of the colour printing process and how printing presses work.

PRINTING's Find Out More line sends you to CHINA, HISTORY OF, which lists ancient Chinese inventions, including printing.

The entry on the history of China is followed by a collection page showing Chinese jewellery and ornaments.

CONTINENT AND COUNTRY PAGES

The encyclopedia contains entries on all the world's continents and countries, each containing a detailed map. Continent entries focus on the physical geography of the region; country entries provide information about the society and economy of the country. Below is the single-page entry on the Netherlands

The country's flag appears by its name.

Locator map

A small map in the top left-hand corner of the page shows you where the region lies within a continent or in relation to the rest of the world.

Map of Netherlands' position in Europe.

The introduction defines the region and provides an overview to the entry.

Compass points north

Scale bar

Scale bar and compass

Each map has a scale bar that shows how distances on the map relate to actual miles and kilometers. The compass shows you which direction on the map is north (N).

Grid reference

The numbers and letters around the map help you find all the places listed in the index.

The index gives Amsterdam's grid reference as C4, so you can find it on the map by locating the third square along (C) and the fourth square down (4).

Population density

A population density diagram shows how many people there are to every square mile or square kilometer.

The Netherlands is a very densely populated country

KEY TO MAP

—— International border	Lake	● Capital city
---- Disputed border	Seasonal lake	◉ Major town
—— Road	River	● Minor town
—— Railroad	Canal	▲ Spot height (feet)
✈ International airport	Waterfall	▼ Spot depth (feet)

NETBALL see BALL GAMES

NETHERLANDS

ALSO CALLED HOLLAND, the Netherlands straddles the deltas of five major rivers in northwest Europe. The Dutch people say they created their own country because they have reclaimed about one-third of the land from sea or marshland by enclosing the area with earth barriers, or dikes, and draining the water from it. Despite being one of the most densely populated countries in the world, the Netherlands enjoys high living standards. Amsterdam is the official capital, although the government is based at The Hague.

NETHERLANDS FACTS

CAPITAL CITY Amsterdam (seat of government The Hague)
AREA 37,330 sq km (14,413 sq miles)
POPULATION 15,800,000
MAIN LANGUAGE Dutch
MAJOR RELIGION Christian
CURRENCY Euro
LIFE EXPECTANCY 78 years
PEOPLE PER DOCTOR 385
GOVERNMENT Multi-party democracy
ADULT LITERACY 99%

Amsterdam
The Dutch capital is built on 70 islands, linked by about 500 bridges, which span its many canals. The best way to get around is by bicycle, around 750,000 people cycle to school or work each day. Today, Amsterdam is a busy centre for tourism and diamond trading.

One of Amsterdam's many canals

People
The Dutch see their society as the most tolerant in Europe, with relaxed laws on sexuality, drugs, and euthanasia. The country has a long history of welcoming immigrants, often from former Dutch colonies. Most of these people are now assimilated as Dutch citizens. However, members of the small Turkish community, which makes up just one per cent of the population, do not have full citizenship.

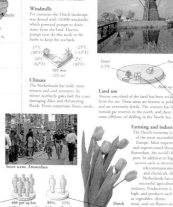

Street scene, Amsterdam

466 per sq km (1,206 per sq mile)

89% Urban

11% Rural

Dutch tulips

Physical features

The Netherlands is mainly flat, with 27 per cent of the land below sea level, and protected from the sea by natural sand dunes along the coast, and by artificial dikes. Wide sandy plains cover most of the rest of the country, falling into a few, low hills in the eastern and southern parts of the country.

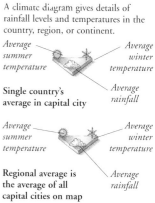

Canals
The Netherlands is a land of canals, which drain the land and serve as waterways for the movement of people and freight. Amsterdam alone has more than 100 canals.

Windmills
For centuries the Dutch landscape was dotted with 10,000 windmills, which powered pumps to drain water from the land. Electric pumps now do this work in the battle to keep the sea back.

37°C (99°F) / -25°C (-13°F)
16°C (62°F) / 2°C (36°F)
580 mm (23 in)

Climate
The Netherlands has mild, rainy winters and cool summers. In winter northerly gales lash the coast, damaging dikes and threatening floods. Frosts sometimes freeze canals.

Forest 3.5%
Farmland 84.5%
Built-up 12%

Land use
Almost one-third of the land has been reclaimed from the sea. These areas are known as polders and are extremely fertile. The country has large natural gas reserves in the north, and there is some offshore oil drilling in the North Sea.

Farming and industry
The Dutch economy is one of the most successful in Europe. Most imports and exports travel through Rotterdam, the world's biggest port. In addition to high-tech sectors such as electronics, telecommunications, and chemicals, the Netherlands has a successful agricultural industry. Productivity is high, and products such as vegetables, cheese, meat, and cut flowers are significant export earners.

FIND OUT MORE — DAMS — EMPIRES — EUROPE — EUROPE, HISTORY OF — EUROPEAN UNION — FARMING — NETHERLANDS, HISTORY OF — PORTS AND WATERWAYS

601

Country file

On each country page there is a fact box containing key details about the country, such as its population, capital city, area, currency, political system, and main language and religion. Other categories of information include:

Literacy – the percentage of people over 15 years old who can read and write.
People per doctor – a rough guide to the availability of medical facilities.
Life expectancy – how long an average person can expect to live.

Climate

A climate diagram gives details of rainfall levels and temperatures in the country, region, or continent.

Average summer temperature / *Average winter temperature*
Average rainfall

Single country's average in capital city

Average summer temperature / *Average winter temperature*
Average rainfall

Regional average is the average of all capital cities on map

Concise explanation of the country's main physical characteristics.

Land use

The land-use diagram tells you how much of the the country's total land area is taken up by, for example, woodland, agriculture, and urban developments such as villages, towns, and cities.

Most of the land in the Netherlands is used for farming.

Urban/rural split

A small diagram shows the percentage of people living in urban (built-up) areas and rural (country) areas.

The majority of people in the Netherlands live in urban areas.

REFERENCE PAGES

Volume 3 of the Encyclopedia contains an illustrated reference section with essential facts, figures, and statistical data, divided into the five main strands described here.

International world

This strand contains a double-page map showing all the countries of the world, and data on the world's population, economy, and resources.

History

The history strand features a timeline of key historical events, stretching from 40,000 BC to the present day, together with the dates of major wars, revolutions, battles, and great leaders.

Living world

The centrepiece of this strand is a detailed guide to the classification of living things, supported by lists of species in danger, and many other facts about the natural world.

People, arts, and media

This strand is crammed full of information about television, theatre, music, art, philosophy, architecture, literature, dance, and much more besides.

Science

A double-page spread on the periodic table is supported by key data on the weather, mathematics, the Earth and the Universe, and measurement conversion tables.

ABORIGINAL AUSTRALIANS

THE ABORIGINALS settled the Australian continent more than 40,000 years ago. They lived in total isolation from the rest of the world, existing by hunting and gathering. In the 18th century, the Europeans arrived, forcing the Aboriginals off their territories. Today, many feel isolated from white society, but still try to preserve their tribal identity.

Some early peoples crossed by means of a land bridge.

Settlers stayed near the coast and rivers where more food was available.

Aboriginal history

Aboriginals first reached Australia during the last Ice Age. Sea levels were low, and they were able to cross from southeast Asia over land bridges and small stretches of water. When the ice melted and sea levels rose again, the continent was completely cut off. Initially, the settlers clung to the coasts and rivers, but gradually moved across the continent. By the time Europeans arrived, there were about 500 different tribal groups living in Australia.

Ways of life

Traditionally, Aboriginals lived by hunting and gathering. They were nomadic, roaming over large stretches of territory, setting up temporary camps near watering places, and moving on when food supplies were exhausted. They traded with other tribes, exchanging goods such as spears.

Hunting and gathering

Aboriginals lived by hunting animals such as kangaroos, and supplemented their diet with wild plants, nuts, and berries. The hunters used spears with stone blades and wooden boomerangs, a type of missile that flies back to the thrower. Some tribes developed an elaborate sign language, so that they could send silent messages to each other when they were stalking game.

Aboriginal hunters used silent signals to avoid disturbing the game. The sign for kangaroo starts with a closed hand and moves to an open shape.

Corroborees

Aboriginal peoples have handed down stories, songs, and traditions from generation to generation. This culture is kept alive at corroborees, ceremonial dances where tribes gather together to retell the tales of Australia's past through songs, music, and dance.

Dreamtime

The Aboriginals believe that Dreamtime is a period when Ancestral Beings shaped the land, creating all species and human beings. These beings are thought to live on eternally in spirit form. Human beings are believed to be a part of nature, closely associated with all other living things. Images of spirits of Dreamtime, such as Lightning Man, cover sacred cliffs and caves in tribal areas.

Barrkinj – wife of Lightning Man

Lightning Man, also known as Namarrgon

Lightning Man was believed to have created thunder and lightning.

Uluru (Ayers Rock)

Aboriginals believe that the Ancestral Beings created the Australian landscape, and established customs and traditions still followed today. They have left evidence of their presence in the many sacred places, such as Uluru in central Australia. This is revered as a sacred place by the local Aranda people. Once called Ayers Rock by the Australian government, the rock regained its Aboriginal name in 1988.

Aboriginals today

European colonists arrived in Australia in 1788, and displaced Aboriginal tribes from their territory. Today, there are about 250,000 Aboriginals in Australia, many of whom live in urban areas. Although there is still discrimination, Aboriginals are beginning to benefit from government aid, and to assert their civil rights.

Land rights

When the Europeans arrived in Australia they claimed that the land was *Terra nullius*, that it belonged to no one, and that they were entitled to occupy it. More recently, the Aboriginals have campaigned to regain their lost territory and sacred sites. In 1993, the Australian government reversed its *Terra nullius* policy.

Education

During early contact with the Europeans, Aboriginal languages were lost or fell into disuse. In 1972, the government established a bilingual education programme. Many children are now taught in their tribal languages before learning English. Books, radio, and television broadcasts are all available in many Aboriginal languages.

FIND OUT MORE   ART, HISTORY OF   AUSTRALASIA AND OCEANIA   AUSTRALIA   AUSTRALIA, HISTORY OF   COOK, JAMES   MYTHS AND LEGENDS   RELIGIONS   SOCIETIES, HUMAN

ACIDS AND ALKALIS

LEMON JUICE AND VINEGAR taste sour because they contain weak acids. An acid is a substance that dissolves in water to form positively charged particles called hydrogen ions (H^+). The opposite of an acid is an alkali, which dissolves in water to form negatively charged ions of hydrogen and oxygen, called hydroxide ions (OH^-). Alkalis are "anti-acids" because they cancel out acidity. Toothpaste, for example, contains an alkali to cancel out acidity in the mouth that would otherwise damage teeth.

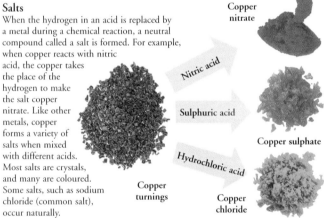

Hydrochloric acid

There is a tremendous fizzing as hydrogen gas is given off.

Zinc replaces the hydrogen in the acid to form zinc chloride.

Zinc nuggets

pH scale

The concentration of hydrogen ions in a solution is known as its pH. Scientists use the pH scale to measure acidity and alkalinity. On the pH scale, a solution with a pH lower than 7 is acidic, and a solution with a pH greater than 7 is alkaline. Water is neutral, with a pH of 7. A solution's pH can be tested with universal indicator solution or paper, which changes colour in acids and alkalis.

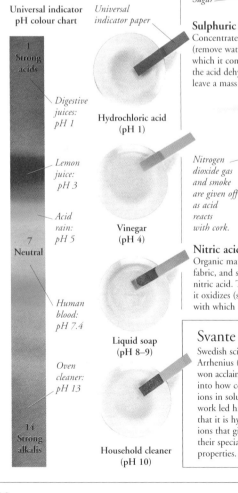

Universal indicator pH colour chart

Universal indicator paper

1 Strong acids

Digestive juices: pH 1

Hydrochloric acid (pH 1)

Lemon juice: pH 3

Acid rain: pH 5

Vinegar (pH 4)

7 Neutral

Human blood: pH 7.4

Liquid soap (pH 8–9)

Oven cleaner: pH 13

Household cleaner (pH 10)

14 Strong alkalis

Strong acids

The more hydrogen ions an acid forms in water, the stronger it is, and the lower its pH. Strong acids, such as sulphuric acid and nitric acid, are very dangerous and must be handled carefully.

Sulphuric acid

Carbon

Sugar

Sulphuric acid
Concentrated sulphuric acid will dehydrate (remove water from) any substance with which it comes into contact. For example, the acid dehydrates sugar, a carbohydrate, to leave a mass of smouldering black carbon.

Cork

Nitrogen dioxide gas and smoke are given off as acid reacts with cork.

Nitric acid

Nitric acid
Organic matter, such as paper, cork, rubber, fabric, and skin, is rapidly decomposed by nitric acid. The acid is so corrosive because it oxidizes (supplies oxygen to) any material with which it comes into contact.

Svante Arrhenius

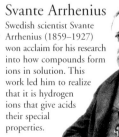

Swedish scientist Svante Arrhenius (1859–1927) won acclaim for his research into how compounds form ions in solution. This work led him to realize that it is hydrogen ions that give acids their special properties.

Acids and metals

Even the weakest acids cannot be stored in metal containers because acids are corrosive to most metals. When an acid reacts with a metal, hydrogen gas is given off and the metal dissolves in the acid to form a compound called a salt. The reaction is very violent with metals such as potassium and sodium, and quite vigorous with metals such as magnesium and zinc.

Salts
When the hydrogen in an acid is replaced by a metal during a chemical reaction, a neutral compound called a salt is formed. For example, when copper reacts with nitric acid, the copper takes the place of the hydrogen to make the salt copper nitrate. Like other metals, copper forms a variety of salts when mixed with different acids. Most salts are crystals, and many are coloured. Some salts, such as sodium chloride (common salt), occur naturally.

Copper nitrate

Nitric acid

Sulphuric acid

Copper sulphate

Hydrochloric acid

Copper turnings

Copper chloride

Acid industry

Acids are widely used in industry because they react so readily with other materials. For example, sulphuric acid is used in the production of dyes and pigments, artificial fibres, plastics, soaps, and explosives. The acid is made by sulphur and oxygen reacting together.

Sulphuric acid chemical plant

Acid rain
Burning fossil fuels to produce energy for use at home and in industry releases polluting gases into the air. The gases dissolve in water in the clouds to form nitric acid and sulphuric acid. This water falls as acid rain, which erodes stone buildings and statues, kills trees and aquatic life, and reduces the soil's fertility.

Bases and alkalis

The acidity of vinegar (ethanoic acid) can be neutralized, or cancelled out, by adding chalk (calcium carbonate). Any substance that neutralizes acidity, such as chalk, is called a base. An alkali is a base that dissolves in water. An alkali's strength is measured by the number of hydroxide ions it forms in water. Strong alkalis, such as sodium hydroxide, are just as corrosive as strong acids.

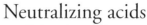

Chalk and vinegar react together and release carbon dioxide gas.

The product of the reaction is a salt called calcium ethanoate.

The mixture spills out of the flask.

Testing the mixture with universal indicator solution proves that it is now neutral – the acidity has been cancelled out.

Soaps and detergents

Alkalis are good at dissolving oil and grease, so they are widely used in the manufacture of soaps and detergents. Most dirt is bound to skin, clothes, or eating utensils by grease. The grease makes it difficult to remove the dirt with water alone, because water and grease do not mix. A soap or detergent, such as washing-up liquid, breaks the grease up into tiny drops and allows the water to wash away the dirt.

Once the washing-up liquid has broken down the grease, the water can wet the plate and dissolve the rest of the dirt.

Oil slicks

Accidents with oil tankers at sea can create huge oil slicks (spillages) on the water's surface. Strong detergents called dispersants may be used to break up the oil. Wildlife experts use weaker detergents, such as washing-up liquid, to clean the feathers of oil-coated seabirds. If the birds' feathers – which usually keep them warm and dry – become clogged with oil, the birds may lose their buoyancy and drown, or die of exposure to the cold.

Batteries

Acids, alkalis, and salts are electrolytes, meaning that they conduct electricity when in solution. Batteries consist of an electrolyte – usually in the form of a moist paste or liquid – between two rods or plates called electrodes. The most common battery is the dry cell, which uses the salt ammonium chloride as an electrolyte. Long-life batteries contain alkaline electrolytes, such as potassium hydroxide; car batteries have electrolytes of sulphuric acid.

Car battery

Long-life battery

Dry cell

Alkali industry

The main raw material in the alkali industry is brine (salt water). Sodium hydroxide, which is used to make soaps and paper, is produced from brine by electrolysis (passing electricity through it). Brine will also absorb carbon dioxide to make sodium carbonate, which is used in textile treatment, photography, and glass making.

Electrolysis of brine to make sodium hydroxide

Neutralizing acids

An alkali and an acid react together to give a neutral salt. In addition, hydroxide ions (OH$^-$) in the alkali combine with the acid's hydrogen ions (H$^+$) to produce water (H$_2$O). In daily life, problems of unwanted acidity are solved by adding an alkali of the appropriate strength.

Soil acidity

The pH of soil varies from area to area. Few crops grow well in highly acidic soil, because the acid dissolves vital minerals that the plants need for healthy growth and allows them to be washed away. Farmers treat acidic soil by spreading lime (calcium oxide) over their fields. This is a cheaply produced alkali made from limestone. It neutralizes the acid in the soil, making it more fertile.

Farmer liming acidic soil

Curing indigestion

The human stomach uses hydrochloric acid to break down food. Some foods cause your stomach to produce so much acid that it gives you discomfort. Stomach powders or indigestion tablets can cure this. They contain weak alkalis that neutralize the acidity, but do not harm your stomach, or react too vigorously with the acid.

Stomach powder fizzes as it reacts with lemon juice (citric acid).

Bee and wasp stings

A bee sting is painful because it is acidic. Treating the sting with a weak alkali, such as soap or bicarbonate of soda, relieves the pain by neutralizing the acid. In contrast, a wasp sting is alkaline, so it can be neutralized by a weak acid, such as vinegar or lemon juice.

Wasp

Bee

Fritz Haber

In 1908, the German chemist Fritz Haber (1868–1934) developed a process for making the alkali ammonia, which is used to make fertilizers and explosives. The Haber process involves reacting nitrogen from the air with hydrogen at high pressure and temperature. Haber later devised a way of making nitric acid by heating ammonia in air.

Timeline

c.600 BC The Phoenicians use alkaline wood ash to make soap.

11th century AD Arab chemists make sulphuric, nitric, and hydrochloric acids.

1780s World's first sulphuric acid factory opens in France.

1865 Ernest Solvay, a Belgian chemist, develops the first commercially successful process for making the alkali, sodium carbonate, on a large scale.

Sodium carbonate

1887 Svante Arrhenius proposes that it is hydrogen ions that give acids their special properties.

1908 Fritz Haber invents a process for making ammonia.

1909 The Danish chemist Søren Sørensen (1868–1939) devises the pH scale.

FIND OUT MORE | ATOMS AND MOLECULES | BEES AND WASPS | CHEMISTRY | DIGESTION | ELECTRICITY | MIXTURES AND COMPOUNDS | POLLUTION | ROCKETS | SOIL

ADVERTISING AND MARKETING

WHEN A COMPANY WISHES TO SELL or improve the sales of its products or services, it may decide to advertise. Newspapers and magazines carry advertisements, as do billboards, television, and radio. Marketing is the wider process of creating a product or service, advertising it, and selling it. Advertising and marketing are vast industries that affect all our lives.

CHANEL

Copy line gives us product information. Here, the tyre-making company Pirelli uses humour and an eye-catching image to advertise its tyres' road-holding ability.

How advertising works

Advertisements use humour and strong images to get our attention. Short, memorable catchphrases called slogans become associated with the product. An advertising campaign often combines posters and television advertisements so that repetition ensures people remember the product.

Well-known athlete

The striking image of an athlete in high heels grabs our attention.

POWER IS NOTHING WITHOUT CONTROL.

Product name

Image

Advertisers try to create a product image that will appeal to particular customers. An advertisement for perfume, for example, may project an image of beauty and sophistication. Well-known personalities may be shown endorsing a product to strengthen its image.

Public relations

Many companies use public relations, or PR, to improve their standing with the people who buy their products. The two main branches of PR are research and communication. Research tries to find out what people think about the company and its products. Companies communicate with people through press coverage, advertising, and sponsorship.

Marketing

A company's marketing strategy includes market research, product development, publicity, advertising, and point of sale displays. The marketing department researches the products people want, and works with other departments to make sure that products meet the customer's needs and expectations.

Pepsi-Cola painted Concorde blue to gain publicity.

Market research

The purpose of market research is to find out what sort of people are likely to buy a product, and what will make them buy one product rather than another. Researchers get this information from interviews, questionnaires, and government statistics.

Point of sale

Shops use posters and display units to encourage people to buy products. Point of sale displays try to catch the customer's eye where he or she can buy the product immediately. Shop window displays aim to draw customers into a shop.

OILILY

Advertising agencies

Companies use advertising agencies to advise them on their advertising strategy. Advertising agencies conduct market research, plan which forms of media the client's advertisements should appear in, and finally prepare the client's advertisements.

The film is combined with a sound track, and then edited.

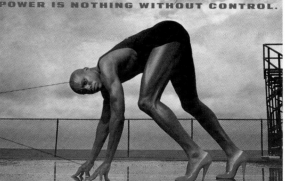

Storyboards

The first stage of producing a television advertisement is to present a storyboard of ideas to the client, showing how the final advertisement will look. A storyboard looks rather like a comic strip, with a series of pictures showing how the action will run. If the client approves the storyboard, production can go ahead.

Production

The advertising agency hires a production team to film the advertisement. This will include a producer, who supervises the rehearsal schedule, and a director, who directs the action when the commercial is being filmed. Once the film has been shot, a sound track is added. The sound track may be a voice-over repeating the product name and a catchy tune called a jingle.

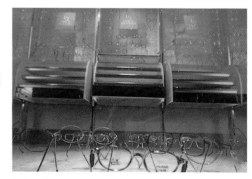

Advertisement

Once the advertisement has been completed, it is shown to the client. If the client approves the film, it is taken to the television stations to be aired. Television advertising is by far the most expensive form of advertising, but it is the most effective since it reaches people in their own homes.

FIND OUT MORE   DESIGN   FILMS AND FILM-MAKING   MONEY   SHOPS   TELEVISION   TRADE AND INDUSTRY

AFRICA

THE SECOND LARGEST CONTINENT after Asia, Africa is dominated in the north by the vast Sahara Desert and in the east by the Great Rift Valley. A belt of rainforest lies along the Equator, and grasslands provide grazing for herds of wild animals. Africa is home to many different peoples, each with their own distinctive languages and customs. Islam and Christianity are widespread, but many Africans adhere to their own traditional beliefs.

Physical features

Most of Africa is a high plateau covered with deserts, lush rainforests, and dry grasslands. It is crossed by rivers, which bring water to dry regions and provide communications. Although they lie on the Equator, the high peaks in the east are snow-capped all year. Africa has several volcanoes.

Sahara

The world's largest desert, the Sahara, covers much of northwestern Africa. It has an area of 9,065,000 sq km (3,263,400 sq miles) and is rapidly expanding as land at its edges is overgrazed. With less than 100 mm (4 in) of rainfall every year and daytime temperatures of up to 50°C (122°F), only a few specially adapted plants and animals survive here.

River Nile

The Nile is the world's longest river. From its source in Lake Victoria, it flows 6,695 km (4,160 miles) north through Uganda, Sudan, and Egypt to the Mediterranean Sea. Africa's third longest river, the Niger, flows 4,180 km (2,597 miles) in a big loop through western Africa, ending in Nigeria in a delta bigger than that of the Nile.

Mountains rise from the Great Rift Valley.

River Nile at Aswan in Egypt

Great Rift Valley

The mountains of Ethiopia are divided by the Great Rift Valley that stretches 6,000 km (3,750 miles) north from Mozambique, through east Africa and the Red Sea, into Syria. The valley is formed by massive cracks in the Earth's crust. It is up to 90 km (55 miles) wide, and in millions of years will eventually divide the African continent.

Simen Mountains, Ethiopia

Okavango Delta

Many rivers end in deltas at the sea, but the Okavango River in southern Africa has a delta that forms a swamp in the Kalahari Desert. The Okavango rises in Angola and flows 974 km (605 miles) to Botswana, where its delta and swamps cover more than 22,000 sq km (8,500 sq miles).

AFRICA FACTS

AREA	30,335,000 sq km (11,712,434 sq miles)
POPULATION	811,600,000
NUMBER OF COUNTRIES	53
BIGGEST COUNTRY	Algeria
SMALLEST COUNTRY	Seychelles
HIGHEST POINT	Kilimanjaro (Tanzania) 5,895 m (19,341 ft)
LONGEST RIVER	Nile (Uganda/Sudan/ Egypt) 6,695 km (4,160 miles)
BIGGEST LAKE	Lake Victoria (East Africa) 68,880 sq km (26,560 sq miles)

Cross-section through Africa

Africa rises sharply from the Atlantic Ocean up to about 1,000 m (3,280 ft) before dropping down into the marshes of the Zaire Basin. The Ruwenzori Mountains and Great Rift Valley lie to the east, and the plateau falls gently to the Indian Ocean.

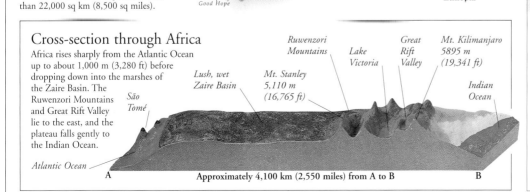

Ruwenzori Mountains

Lake Victoria

Great Rift Valley

Mt. Kilimanjaro 5895 m (19,341 ft)

Lush, wet Zaire Basin

Mt. Stanley 5,110 m (16,765 ft)

São Tomé

Indian Ocean

Atlantic Ocean

A   Approximately 4,100 km (2,550 miles) from A to B   B

Map labels: Mediterranean Sea, Madeira (Portugal), MOROCCO, TUNISIA, Gulf of Sirte, Nile Delta, Qattara Depression, Suez Canal, Canary Is. (Spain), ALGERIA, LIBYA, EGYPT, Libyan Desert, Red Sea, ASIA, WESTERN SAHARA (Occupied by Morocco), Tropic of Cancer, Ahaggar 2918m, Tibesti 3145m, Nubian Desert, MAURITANIA, MALI, NIGER, CHAD, SUDAN, ERITREA, L. Chad, Blue Nile, White Nile, DJIBOUTI, Gulf of Aden, Assal 156m, GAMBIA, SENEGAL, GUINEA-BISSAU, BURKINA, NIGERIA, Benue, Ethiopian Highlands, 4620m Kirinyaga, ETHIOPIA, Shebeli, SIERRA LEONE, GUINEA, IVORY COAST, GHANA, BENIN, TOGO, CENTRAL AFRICAN REPUBLIC, Sudd, Elemi Triangle, SOMALIA, LIBERIA, Niger Delta, CAMEROON, Ubangi, L. Turkana, ATLANTIC OCEAN, EQUATORIAL GUINEA, SAO TOME & PRINCIPE, Congo, UGANDA, KENYA, Equator, GABON, CONGO, DEM. REP. CONGO, Congo Basin, Mt Stanley 5110m, L. Victoria, 5200m, RWANDA, BURUNDI, Kilimanjaro 5895m, Pemba, Zanzibar, Cabinda (Angola), Kasai, TANZANIA, L. Tanganyika, SEYCHELLES, L. Nyasa, COMOROS, ANGOLA, ZAMBIA, MALAWI, Mayotte (France), Victoria Falls 108m, Zambezi, L. Kariba, MOZAMBIQUE, Mozambique Channel, MADAGASCAR, NAMIBIA, Okavango Delta, ZIMBABWE, 2658m, BOTSWANA, Kalahari Desert, Namib Desert, SWAZILAND, Orange, INDIAN OCEAN, SOUTH AFRICA, LESOTHO 3482m, Orange, Drakensberg, Cape of Good Hope, Tropic of Capricorn

Scale: 0 km 1000, 0 miles 1000

Climatic zones

Although most of Africa is warm or hot all year round, the climate varies greatly because of the wide range of landscapes. Parts of the north coast have hot, dry summers and cooler, moist winters. Desert regions have cold nights, scorching hot days, and almost no rain at all. On the Equator the climate is hot and humid, with high rainfall. Mountain regions have warm summers and cool winters.

Scrubland *Desert* *Grassland* *Tropical rainforest* *Wetland* *Mountain*

Fantastically shaped dunes are formed by strong desert winds.

Scrubland

Much of the northern coast of Africa has a warm Mediterranean climate. Coastal cliffs and hills are covered in sparse, low-growing, often fragrant plants and shrubs that are able to thrive in the poor, stony soils. Many of the plants have thorns and small, leathery leaves to prevent them from drying out in the fierce heat of the sun and frequent sea breezes.

Baie de Souhalias, Algeria

Evergreen plants are able to retain their moisture in the heat.

Savannah

About 40 per cent of Africa is covered with savannah, which is the name given to grassland with scattered trees and shrubs. This type of land forms a wide loop around the Zaire (Congo) Basin. Vast herds of grazing animals, such as antelopes and zebras, move around the savannah seeking fresh grass to eat.

Masai Mara, Kenya

Deserts

About 40 per cent of Africa is desert. The Erg of Bilma in Niger is part of the vast Sahara. In Arabic, *erg* means a sandy expanse. The sand is blown by the wind into ripples and into huge dunes, some of which may be nearly 200 m (650 ft) high. Two other main desert areas are the Kalahari and the Namib, both in southern Africa.

Occasional stunted trees offer animals some protection from the harsh sun.

Many streams and rivers cross the rainforest.

Low shrubs cover some of the mountains' lower slopes and foothills.

Tropical rainforest

Dense, tropical rainforest covers less than 20 per cent of Africa. The most extensive areas lie close to the Equator in West Africa and in Central Africa's Zaire (Congo) Basin. Thousands of species of tree flourish in the hot, humid climate, which produces rain all year round. However, large-scale felling of trees for timber hardwoods, such as teak and mahogany, threatens to destroy this environment.

Mahogany leaf

Mountain

Africa's highest ranges include the Drakensberg, in southeast Africa, which runs for about 1,130 km (70 miles) through South Africa and Lesotho and forms part of the rim of the great South African Plateau. The highest point is Thabana Ntlenyana at 3,482 m (11,424 ft). Even higher mountain ranges are the Atlas range in Morocco, and the Ruwenzori on the border between Uganda and Congo (Zaire).

People

One in eight of the world's people lives in Africa, mostly along the north and west coasts, and in the fertile river valleys. Although traditionally people live in small villages, a growing number are moving to towns and cities to look for work. Birth rates in many countries are high and families are large. About half the population is under 15 years old.

Ghanaian girls   Tanzanian girl   Egyptian boy

Resources

Africa has many resources, but they are unevenly distributed. Libya and Nigeria are leading oil producers, southern Africa is rich in gold and diamonds, and Zambia is a leading copper producer. Tropical forests yield valuable timber but are being felled at an alarming rate. Africa is a leading producer of cocoa beans, cassava, bananas, coffee, and tea.

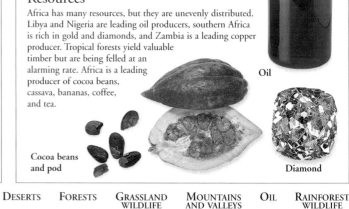

Oil

Cocoa beans and pod

Diamond

FIND OUT MORE   AFRICA, HISTORY OF   AFRICAN WILDLIFE   CLIMATES   CONTINENTS   DESERTS   FORESTS   GRASSLAND WILDLIFE   MOUNTAINS AND VALLEYS   OIL   RAINFOREST WILDLIFE

AFRICA, HISTORY OF

CIVILIZATION IN AFRICA BEGAN TO appear more than 5,000 years ago with the rise of ancient Egypt. From about 2,500 years ago in sub-Saharan Africa, many other different kingdoms also developed. The Sahara acted as a barrier to keep this area separate from the rest of the world until the arrival of Arab traders in the 8th century. From the 15th century, the arrival of Europeans, the subsequent slave trade, and European imperialism had a profound effect on the continent. Since the 1950s, all African nations have reclaimed independence, although modern Africa continues to struggle with its post-colonial legacy and environmental problems.

Ancient empires

North Africa was in a good position to trade with western Asia. This caused rich empires to develop, including Meroë (modern Sudan, c.600 BC–AD 350), and Aksum (a trading state in northern Ethiopia, c.100 BC–AD 1000). Ghana (in West Africa, c.500–1300) developed for similar reasons.

Meroë
From the city of Meroë, the Kushites controlled trade in the Red Sea and the Nile River from 600 BC. They exported luxury goods, such as ostrich feathers and leopard skins, and built fine temples and flat-topped pyramids over the graves of their dead.

Ruined temple, Meroë

Ghana
Ghana (located on the borders of modern Mali and Mauritania), one of Africa's most important empires, controlled the trans-Saharan trade in gold. Ghana's kings wore gold jewellery, and gold-embroidered clothes and turbans. Surviving gold artefacts show the incredible wealth of this kingdom.

Heads of gold, often of royalty, played an important part in rituals.

Carving was made of wood and coated with gold.

Head weighs 1.5 kg (3 lbs).

Figures were attached to royal thrones.

Bird ornament

Rings were often decorated with flowers.

Finger rings

Stela, Aksum

Aksum
From c.300, Egyptian scholars introduced Christianity to Aksum, which then became famous as a holy city. During this period, Aksum took over the empire based at Meroë. Aksum's people built tall, stone stelae (monuments) to mark the tombs of dead kings.

Early inhabitants

Humans have inhabited Africa for 4 million years. The Sahara was once a fertile land rich in plants and animals. But thousands of years ago, it dried up, and people moved south to the savannah to farm there.

Vegetable dye

Animals

Painted bone

Rock paintings
Rock and bone pictures often depicted everyday events, such as dancing, hunting animals, and fishing. Painters used animal fat coloured with vegetable dyes.

Nok culture
The earliest evidence of Iron Age settlement is called the Nok culture (500 BC–AD 200), which existed in what is now central Nigeria. Nok people lived in farming communities. They made iron weapons and tools for farming, and also produced fine terracotta sculptures.

Terracotta head, Nok culture

Spread of religions

From the 8th century, trade, conquests, and colonialism spread religions such as Islam in Africa. In North Africa, Islam completely replaced traditional religions, which often included the worship of ancestors.

Festival mask

Ancestor worship
In many parts of Africa, communities had sacred shrines where they placed offerings for the spirits of their dead ancestors. Today, during certain annual festivals, members of the community wear special masks, sing, dance, and tell stories in honour of their ancestors.

Islam
By c.800, Middle Eastern Arabs had taken Islam to North Africa. From the 11th century, trade helped spread Islam across the Sahara into West Africa and up the River Nile into Sudan.

Ait Benhaddou, Morocco

Slave trade
By the 1470s, the Portuguese were trading copper, brass, gold, and slaves with Benin in West Africa. In the 1480s, the Portuguese arrived in the islands of Principe and São Tomé in the Gulf of Guinea, just off the west African coast. They established sugar plantations, and forced African captives (mainly kidnapped in Senegal and Gambia) to work as slaves on the plantations. This was the beginning of European domination in Africa.

Plaque showing Portuguese soldier, 1500s

A

Colonialism

During the 1800s, Europeans colonized areas in Africa, introducing Christianity, and taking economic control. They used African workers to grow or mine precious raw materials, but sent the materials to be manufactured in Europe and America – where profits stayed. During this period, slavery was at its height as Europeans kidnapped Africans to work in the Americas.

African carving of a European

African Diaspora

The slave trade scattered more than 20 million Africans throughout the Americas and Europe, undermining African culture in the process. Over the centuries, the dispersed descendents of these slaves became known as the African Diaspora.

Christianity

Europe sent missionaries to Africa to set up schools and churches, and to convert Africans to Christianity. They also tried to abolish African traditional religions, often punishing those who still practised them.

Traditional witch doctors

Voodoo voice disguiser

Voodoo

In 19th-century Caribbean colonies, traditional ancestor worship combined with Christianity to produce a religion called voodoo.

Carving of Queen Victoria

Scramble for Africa

In 1884, European leaders decided that their countries could claim African territories as colonies when occupied by Europeans. This started a scramble to the interior in search of new lands. By 1902, all of Africa was colonized, except Liberia and Ethiopia.

French
British
German
Portuguese
Belgium
Spanish
Italian
Anglo-Egyptian

Morocco Tunisia
Algeria Libya Egypt
Liberia Nigeria British Somaliland
Sierra Leone Ethiopia
British East Africa (Kenya)
Angola

World Wars I and II

Although both world wars were European, thousands of Africans lost their lives as colonial rulers forced them to join the army. One cause of World War I was German resentment against other European countries during colonization. In World War II, North Africa became a battleground, as German and Italian forces invaded British- and French-ruled territories.

Troops at El Alamein, Egypt

World War I

When World War I broke out in 1914, the Ottoman Empire controlled North Africa. The Egyptians colluded with the British to overthrow Turkish rule, and they were helped from 1916 to 1918 by the eccentric soldier and author Thomas Edward Lawrence (1888–1935), who became famous as Lawrence of Arabia. After the war, Egypt became a British protectorate but signed a treaty for independence in 1922.

El Alamein

In 1941, Italian and German forces invaded North African territories held by the British. The British recruited soldiers from their colonies of Nigeria, Ghana, and Sierra Leone to join the fight on their behalf. In 1942, the British defeated the Germans at the historic battle of El Alamein. This battle was a turning point in the war.

Herero and Nama tribes fight German colonialists, Namibia, 1904

African resistance

Africans strenuously resisted colonialism. The Ethiopians fought to stay independent and won (1896); Zimbabwe and Sudan rebelled against the British (1896 and 1920); tribes in Angola tried to overthrow the Portuguese (1902); in Namibia and Tanzania, thousands were killed in uprisings against the Germans (1904–1908); and in Nigeria, tribes revolted against French rule (1920s).

TE Lawrence

African Front

Operation Torch

In 1942, American and British soldiers landed in Morocco and Algeria in an invasion called Operation Torch. Joined by the French, the Allies attacked the German and Italian armies, forcing them into Tunisia. After a bloody battle, Germany's Afrika Korps surrendered. The war on African soil was over by May 1943.

Haile Selassie

Emperor Haile Selassie of Ethiopia (r.1930–74) led his troops against the Italian invasion of 1935. The Italians forced the emperor into exile in 1936, but he returned in 1941. Haile Selassie instituted reforms, suppressed slavery, and worked with the Organization of African Unity. In 1974, the army overthrew the emperor, installing military rule. He died in exile in 1975 aged 84.

Ghanaian
Independence
Day stamps

Independence

After World War II, many Africans wanted to end colonial rule, and govern their own countries. Colonial powers such as France, Portugal, and Britain fought to prevent this, and there were bloody wars of independence in Algeria, Mozambique, Angola, and Zimbabwe. By the late 1960s most African countries had gained independence, but political and economic problems remained.

Returning refugees, Angola

Gold Coast

One of the first colonies to become independent was the former British colony of the Gold Coast. After World War II, anti-colonial feeling had intensified, and, in 1957, the state of Ghana (which was named after a powerful West African medieval empire) became independent. A leading nationalist, Kwame Nkrumah (1909–72) became the new country's first prime minister. In 1960, Nkrumah declared Ghana a republic and himself president for life. He became increasingly dictatorial, while drawing ever further away from the west. In 1966, a police-military coup overthrew Nkrumah.

OAU member states now number 50.

OAU summit, Tunisia

Organization of African Unity

In 1963, the heads of 30 independent African states met to form the OAU (Organization of African Unity). Its aim was to promote political and economic co-operation between the states, and help colonies achieve independence.

Angola War

In 1961, Angola's people rose in revolt against the Portuguese colonial government. The Portuguese army crushed the rebels, who fled into exile in Zaire. While in exile, the rebels formed liberation movements, and waged guerrilla warfare in Angola. In 1974, the liberation forces staged a military uprising, and overthrew the Portuguese, who finally granted independence in 1975. After independence, a bitter civil war erupted between two political groups, both of whom wanted to govern Angola. One side was backed by South African troops, the other by Russian troops. The Angolan factions agreed to a ceasefire in 1994.

Apartheid

By the 1980s, only South Africa was still trying to retain white-minority power. The white government had passed the Apartheid (separateness) Policy in 1948, which classified people according to race. Under apartheid, those classified as Black, Coloured, or Asian had few rights. Apartheid was abolished in 1994.

A taxi stand for whites, South Africa, 1967

Electronics technician

Game park, Kenya

Modern Africa

Mineral-rich Africa has a thriving mining industry. More recently, new African electronics plants are specializing in the assembly of imported electronic components.

Tourism

A century ago, East African governments established game reserves and parks to protect wildlife from hunters. Today, tourists pay to stay in the parks and go on safari to see the wild animals. Kenya now makes more money from tourism than from any other source.

Village co-operatives

Agricultural workers (mainly women) set up village co-operatives to grow food crops, which they sell at the local market. This reverses a situation that existed under colonial governments, when small-scale farmers were forced to grow cash crops (coffee, groundnuts, cocoa, and cotton) to sell to large European companies. The farmers could not grow food crops for themselves, and had to buy expensive imports, such as rice.

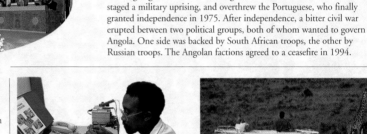

Women's agricultural co-operative, Niger

Women are the main agricultural workers.

Food crops

Deforestation, Somalia

Environmental devastation

In semi-arid areas of Africa, such as Somalia, land is gradually turning into desert. Since the 1950s, there has been a fall in the average annual rainfall, and much of the land has become very dry. The people have often over-used the land for cash crops, and cut down the trees for firewood.

Ken Saro-Wiwa

Ken Saro-Wiwa (1941–1995), a human rights campaigner, was hanged along with eight others by Nigeria's military government. His "crime" was to speak out against the pollution of tribal lands by government-backed international oil companies.

Timeline

African carving

2500 BC Climatic changes in the Sahara region force people to move southward.

c.600 BC Kushite people of Sudan expand and base their capital at Meroë.

c.AD 320–25 King Ezama of Aksum becomes Christian.

500–1300 The kingdom of Ghana controls trans-Saharan trade.

641 Arabs conquer Egypt, and convert it to Islam.

600s The empire based at Aksum begins to decline.

1497 Portuguese explorers land on east coast, after sailing around Africa.

1900 Most of the Sahara region comes under French colonial rule.

1940 Italian forces invade North Africa; Germans follow one year later.

1945 League of Arab States is founded; it includes eight African nations.

1973–75 Horn of Africa suffers a severe drought.

1994–95 In Rwanda 800,000 Hutus are massacred by Tutsis; millions flee the country.

FIND OUT MORE   BENIN EMPIRE   GREAT ZIMBABWE   MALI EMPIRE   MANDELA, NELSON   RELIGIONS   SLAVERY   SONGHAI EMPIRE   SOUTH AFRICA, HISTORY OF

AFRICA, CENTRAL

THE EQUATOR RUNS THROUGH Central Africa, affecting not only climate but also ways of life. There are ten countries. All were European colonies with a history of a cruel slave trade. Although these countries were all independent by the end of the 1960s, they have experienced mixed fortunes. Cameroon is stable, while Democratic Republic of the Congo and the Central African Republic, have suffered dictatorships. Most Central Africans live by farming.

Physical features

The landscape varies according to its distance from the Equator. Much of the region is rolling hills and valleys, with craggy mountains in the north and east. The arid Sahara desert and Sahel cover the extreme north. Farther south, is the vast equatorial basin of the River Congo, surrounded by some unspoilt tropical rainforest.

Dry woodland
Tropical rainforests give way to woodland, where the climate is much drier. Acacia and baobab trees grow in this region. The baobabs have very thick trunks that can hold water to feed themselves. Some baobabs on Cameroon's central plateau live for 1,000 years.

Tibesti
The dramatic cliffs of the volcanic Tibesti Mountains dominate the border between Chad and Libya, in the Sahara Desert. At 3,415 m (11,204 ft) above sea-level, Emi Koussi is the highest peak.

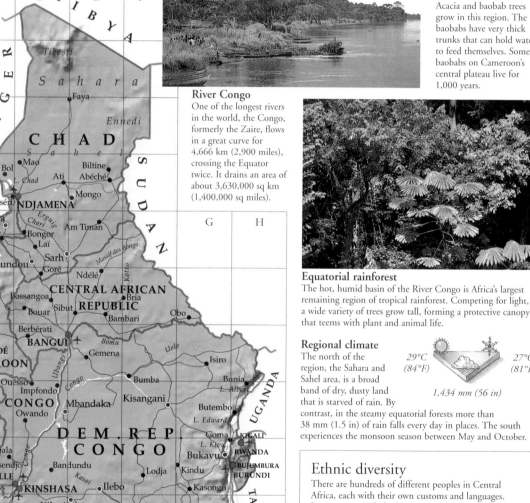

River Congo
One of the longest rivers in the world, the Congo, formerly the Zaire, flows in a great curve for 4,666 km (2,900 miles), crossing the Equator twice. It drains an area of about 3,630,000 sq km (1,400,000 sq miles).

Equatorial rainforest
The hot, humid basin of the River Congo is Africa's largest remaining region of tropical rainforest. Competing for light, a wide variety of trees grow tall, forming a protective canopy that teems with plant and animal life.

Regional climate
The north of the region, the Sahara and Sahel area, is a broad band of dry, dusty land that is starved of rain. By contrast, in the steamy equatorial forests more than 38 mm (1.5 in) of rain falls every day in places. The south experiences the monsoon season between May and October.

29°C (84°F)   27°C (81°F)

1,434 mm (56 in)

Ethnic diversity
There are hundreds of different peoples in Central Africa, each with their own customs and languages. Large groups include the Kongo and Luba, and there are several pygmy groups including the Twa, BaKa, and Mbuti, who live in clearings deep in the rainforests. A growing number of people are moving to towns to escape war, drought, or famine, and because larger centres offer more jobs and food.

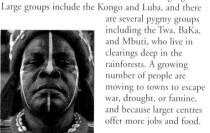

Village chief, Brazzaville, Congo

Chad

The land-locked republic of Chad is one of the world's poorest countries. Nearly half of the land is desert or lies in the Sahel, where rainfall is erratic. More than half of the people work on farmland near the Chari river in the south, but lack of food is still a problem. Chad has some valuable mineral deposits, but they are unexploited.

Muslim nomads
More than 100,000 nomadic Muslims live in the desert and northern Sahel regions of Chad. They include the Kanimbo people, who are related to the Arabs and Berbers of North Africa. Every day, Kanimbo women must walk long distances in the heat to fetch water for their families.

Camels
One of the only ways to cross the vast Sahara Desert is by camel. Camels are used as pack animals to transport forest products and minerals from Lake Chad, as well as for farming, pumping water, and carrying people. Herders value their milk, meat, and hides.

Dried gourds used as bowls for making butter.

Fulani
Throughout Africa a nomadic group called the Fulani herd cattle and roam wherever there is grazing land. They drink the cows' milk and use it to make butter and cheese. Bottle-shaped gourds, a type of fruit, are dried and decorated for use as water carriers and bowls.

CHAD FACTS

CAPITAL CITY N'Djamena

AREA 1,284,000 sq km (495,752 sq miles)

POPULATION 8,100,000

MAIN LANGUAGES French, Arabic, Sara

MAJOR RELIGIONS Muslim, Christian, traditional beliefs

CURRENCY CFA franc

Cameroon

On Africa's west coast, Cameroon was once a colony divided between the French and the British. The two parts gained independence and became a united country in 1961. Despite initial troubles, Cameroon now has one of the most successful economies in Africa, exporting oil, bauxite, and a range of natural products, including cocoa, coffee, and rubber. The country has a diverse culture with more than 230 ethnic groups.

Timber
Like many other African countries, Cameroon sells hardwood logs, including mahogany, ebony, and teak from its rainforests to earn foreign currency. Although the trade represents one tenth of the country's total exports, it poses a serious threat to the future of the forests.

Dried gourds amplify sounds made by strings.

Music
Makossa is a popular style of African folk music that originated in Cameroon. It is played on traditional instruments, including this one, known as a *mvet*. It is made using a wooden stick, horsehair strings, and hollowed-out gourds. *Mvet* players are specially trained and highly regarded in the community.

Several strings are stretched along the stick and plucked to make a range of sounds.

Football
One of Cameroon's leading amateur sports, football is widely enjoyed and people play it whenever they have time. Games draw large crowds of spectators. Cameroon's national football team was acclaimed as one of the best in Africa, after displaying its skills in the 1990 World Cup.

CAMEROON FACTS

CAPITAL CITY Yaoundé

AREA 475,400 sq km (183,567 sq miles)

POPULATION 15,200,000

MAIN LANGUAGES French, English, Fang, Duala, Fulani

MAJOR RELIGIONS Traditional beliefs, Christian, Muslim

CURRENCY CFA franc

Central African Republic

Lying in the very heart of Africa, the Central African Republic, or CAR, has a complicated history. Drought and 13 years of repressive government have made the CAR one of the poorest nations in the world. Only two per cent of the people live in the semi-arid north, and the majority are clustered in villages in the southern rainforests.

Bantu woman

People
Seven major Bantu language groups and many smaller ones make up the population of the CAR. Several thousand hunter-gatherers live in the rainforests in harmony with nature. They survive by eating forest fruits and build their homes from banana leaves.

Cotton
Coffee and cotton together form about 13 per cent of the country's exports. Grown on large plantations, all parts of the cotton plant are used. The fibre, known as a boll, is spun into yarn to make fabric. The seed's oil forms the base of many foods, whilst the plant's stalks and leaves are ploughed back into the soil to fertilize it.

Food
The people of the CAR grow nearly all their own food by subsistence farming. Root crops, such as cassava, yams, and vegetables, are cultivated alongside grains including millet, maize, and sorghum. Fish from the CAR's rivers, including the Chari and Ubangi, is a vital source of protein.

After drying in the sun, cotton bolls are sorted by hand.

Millet

Cassava

CENTRAL AFRICAN REPUBLIC FACTS

CAPITAL CITY Bangui

AREA 622,984 sq km (240,534 sq miles)

POPULATION 3,800,000

MAIN LANGUAGES French, Sango, Zande, Banda, Sara, Arabic

MAJOR RELIGIONS Traditional beliefs, Christian, Muslim

CURRENCY CFA franc

A

Congo

The Republic of Congo was a French territory until 1960. It is a hot, humid land, and its densely forested north has few inhabitants. Nearly half the country's people are members of the Kongo group; the rest include Batéké, M'Bochi, and Sangha. The mineral and timber industries have made Congo wealthy, but many people are still subsistence farmers, growing barely enough food to survive.

Animal skin is stretched across the drum.

Drum

An essential part of African life, drums are used for signalling as well as for music. Most drums are intricately carved out of a solid piece of wood and can be decorated with different woods and hides. Drums are made in all shapes and sizes – this one is almost as tall as the player.

Each cocoa pod contains about 30 beans, for use in chocolate and cosmetics.

Coffee beans

Cocoa pods

Crops
About 50 per cent of the work-force are farmers who grow cassava, maize, rice, peanuts, and fruit to feed their families. Much food is imported. The steady export of coffee and cocoa beans has saved Congo from economic problems.

CONGO FACTS

CAPITAL CITY Brazzaville

AREA 342,000 sq km (132,046 sq miles)

POPULATION 3,100,000

MAIN LANGUAGES French, Kongo

MAJOR RELIGIONS Christian, traditional beliefs

CURRENCY CFA franc

Industry
Oil from the Atlantic Ocean accounts for 90 per cent of Congo's exports, contributing largely to the country's wealth. Fluctuating oil prices have caused some economic problems, but Congo's crop exports have remained strong. The felling of forests to export tropical timber is a pressing environmental concern. Huge barges on the Congo and other rivers carry timber goods as far as Brazzaville; from there the Congo Ocean Railway takes them to Pointe Noire, Congo's only port.

Gabon

A palm-fringed sandy coastline 800 km (500 miles) long, and lush tropical vegetation dominate Gabon's landscape. The country earns 80 per cent of its foreign currency from oil and also sells timber, manganese, and uranium ore. Gabon has the potential to be wealthy, but mismanagement by the government has led to continued poverty.

Libreville
The bustling port city of Libreville was founded in 1849 by French naval officers. Meaning "free town" in French, Libreville was a new home for liberated slaves. It is now a modern, growing city, and a centre of culture, industry, and government. Many citizens are wealthy, but poverty still exists.

GABON FACTS

CAPITAL CITY Libreville

AREA 267,667 sq km (103,346 sq miles)

POPULATION 1,300,000

MAIN LANGUAGES French, Fang

MAJOR RELIGION Christian

CURRENCY CFA franc

Woman in Libreville, Gabon's capital

People
Although Gabon is one of Africa's most thinly populated countries, it contains more than 40 different ethnic groups. The indigenous Fang people form the largest group. Once fierce warriors, they now dominate the government. Most Gabonese people are Christians, and about 90 per cent of their children attend primary schools. The Gabonese traditions of dance, song, poetry, and story-telling remain an important social and cultural part of everyday life.

The Trans-Gabon Railway runs from Libreville to Franceville.

Trans-Gabon Railway
Opened in 1986 to transport gold and manganese, the Trans-Gabon Railway has caused much controversy because it cut through rainforest, destroying many valuable and rare trees.

Equatorial Guinea

Two former Spanish colonies make up the country of Equatorial Guinea, located close to the Equator. Río Muni, also called Mbini, is on mainland Africa, and Bioko Island, which has fertile, volcanic soil that is ideal for growing cocoa beans, is situated to the northwest, off the coast of neighbouring Cameroon.

Traditional healing
Like other Africans, many people in Equatorial Guinea believe that illness is due to the influence of bad spirits. Professional healers use dancing and chants to drive out the evil spirits. They keep a range of animal bones, shells, sticks, and other plant parts in their medicine bags for use in group ceremonies.

Hippopotamus tooth

Cowrie shell

Tree root

Animal bone

Extended families
Among the people of Equatorial Guinea there is a strong tradition of large, extended families, who stay together and help one another in times of hardship.

EQUATORIAL GUINEA FACTS

CAPITAL CITY Malabo

AREA 28,051 sq km (10,830 sq miles)

POPULATION 470,000

MAIN LANGUAGES Spanish, Bubi, Fang, French

MAJOR RELIGION Christian

CURRENCY CFA franc

Dem. Rep. Congo

Formerly known as Belgian Congo and then as Zaire, this country was renamed Democratic Republic of the Congo in 1997 after the overthrow of the corrupt military government. The country consists of a plateau 1,200 m (3,900 ft) above sea-level, through which the River Congo flows. The land is fertile and rich in minerals, but spendthrift governments and civil war, including conflict with Rwanda in 1996–97, have kept it poor.

Cowrie shells are sewn on to decorate the mask.

Mask
Among the many peoples of Dem. Rep. Congo are the Kuba, a small ethnic group who have lived there for many years. Their chief wears a hunting mask, known as a Mashamboy mask, made of shells, beads, and raffia, to symbolize the power of the Great Spirit.

A

DEM. REP. CONGO FACTS

CAPITAL CITY	Kinshasa
AREA	2,345,410 sq km (905,563 sq miles)
POPULATION	52,500,000
MAIN LANGUAGES	French, English, Kiswahili, Lingala
MAJOR RELIGIONS	Christian, traditional beliefs
CURRENCY	Congolese franc

Creole woman selling diamonds

Farming
Dem. Rep. Congo has much potentially cultivable land. Sixty per cent of the population are subsistence farmers, producing palm oil, coffee, tea, rubber, cotton, fruit, vegetables, and rice. Here, on the border of volcanic Virunga National Park, the land is rich and fertile.

Mining
Copper ore, cobalt, and diamonds provide 85 per cent of national exports. Dem. Rep. Congo rates second in world diamond exports, with most mining activity in the Shaba province.

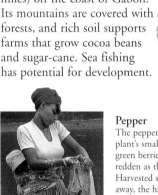

River ports
The River Congo and its tributaries give the country 11,500 km (7,000 miles) of navigable waterways. There are many river ports with boat-building and repair yards, craft shops, and lively markets that sell cassava, fruits, and fish, and delicacies such as monkey and snake meat. Traders take their produce to sell at river markets in dug-out canoes made by local craftsmen.

Ethnic strife
The present country boundaries in Central Africa date back to European colonialism, and cut across logical ethnic groupings. In some places there is actual ethnic warfare, for example that between the Hutus and the Tutsis of Rwanda and Burundi. For hundreds of years, Rwanda was dominated by the Tutsis, who ruled the Hutus. In 1959, the Hutus rebelled, and widespread fighting broke out. In the mid-1990s the violence escalated, resulting in 800,000 Hutu deaths and a massive refugee exodus into other countries.

Refugee camp, Tanzania

Sao Tome and Principe

This tiny country, formed by the main volcanic islands of Sao Tome and Principe, and four smaller islands, lies 200 km (120 miles) off the coast of Gabon. Its mountains are covered with forests, and rich soil supports farms that grow cocoa beans and sugar-cane. Sea fishing has potential for development.

Pepper
The pepper plant's small, green berries redden as they ripen. Harvested straight away, the half-ripe berries are cleaned, dried in the sun, ground, and sifted to make ground black pepper.

Rwanda

One of Africa's most densely populated countries, Rwanda has been made poor by ethnic strife that forced hundreds of thousands of people to flee to Dem. Rep. Congo for safety. Rwanda makes its money by exporting coffee, tea, and tin and tungsten ores. Most of its people just manage to feed themselves.

Burundi

Like Rwanda, its neighbour, Burundi has been torn by conflict between the Tutsis and the Hutus, which has led to riots and thousands of deaths. Burundi has massive oil and nickel reserves beneath Lake Tanganyika, but lacks the funds to begin extraction. Most people are subsistence farmers.

Creole culture
Nobody lived on these islands until Portuguese explorers landed in 1470. The Portuguese peopled the islands with slaves from the mainland. Their mixed descendants created a culture called creole, but the creoles now number only ten per cent because more than 4,000 left the country at independence.

Volcanoes Park
The *Parc des volcans* is a scenic reserve dominated by volcanic mountains, two of which are active. The park is the last refuge of the mountain gorillas, which now number around 630.

RWANDA FACTS

CAPITAL CITY	Kigali
AREA	26,338 sq km (10,169 sq miles)
POPULATION	7,900,000
MAIN LANGUAGES	Kinyarwanda, French, Kiswahili
MAJOR RELIGIONS	Christian, traditional beliefs
CURRENCY	Rwanda Franc

Farming
Most farmers grow cassava and maize to feed their families. Some grow coffee, tea, cotton, and bananas for export. Overplanting fertile land is causing soil erosion.

BURUNDI FACTS

CAPITAL CITY	Bujumbura
AREA	27,830 sq km (10,745 sq miles)
POPULATION	6,500,000
MAIN LANGUAGES	Kirundi, French, Swahili
MAJOR RELIGIONS	Christian, traditional beliefs
CURRENCY	Burundi Franc

SAO TOME AND PRINCIPE FACTS

CAPITAL CITY	São Tomé
AREA	1001 sq km (386 sq miles)
POPULATION	159,900
MAIN LANGUAGE	Portuguese
MAJOR RELIGION	Christian
CURRENCY	Dobra

FIND OUT MORE | AFRICA, HISTORY OF | EMPIRES | FARMING | FORESTS | MONKEYS AND OTHER PRIMATES | MUSIC | OIL | PORTS AND WATERWAYS | SLAVERY | TRAINS AND RAILWAYS

AFRICA, EAST

ONE OF THE WORLD'S OLDEST civilizations, Egypt, occupies the northeastern corner of East Africa, while Kenya, Tanzania, and Uganda sit farther south. Along the Horn of Africa, a piece of land that juts out into the Indian Ocean, are four of the world's poorest countries – Eritrea, Somalia, Ethiopia, and Djibouti. In recent years, Somalia, Sudan, and Ethiopia have been devastated by drought and war. Most East Africans scrape a living from farming, and some rely on food aid from abroad.

Physical features

Running through eastern Africa is the Great Rift Valley, a huge gash in the Earth that continues north through the Red Sea. Other features include the Nile, the world's longest river, and Lake Victoria, Africa's largest lake. The varied landscape includes deserts, grassland, mountains, and swamps.

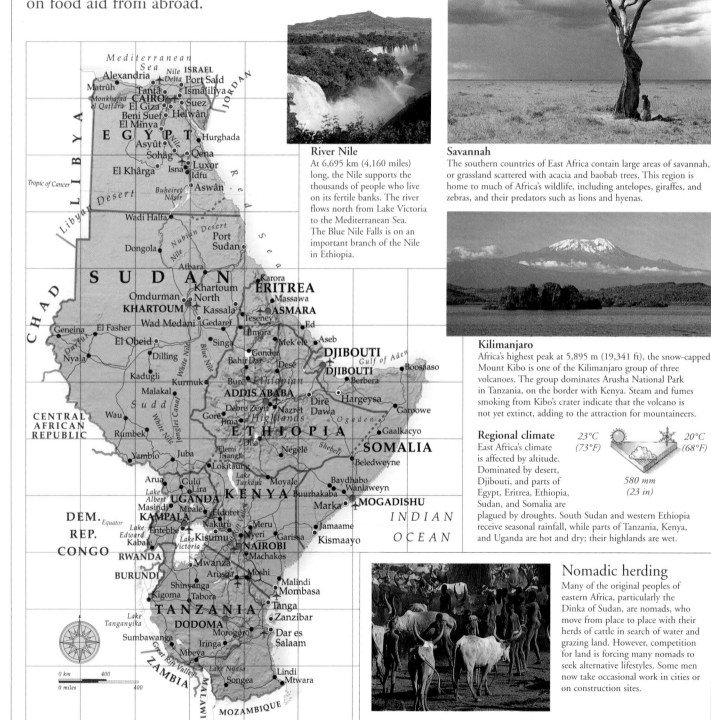

River Nile
At 6,695 km (4,160 miles) long, the Nile supports the thousands of people who live on its fertile banks. The river flows north from Lake Victoria to the Mediterranean Sea. The Blue Nile Falls is on an important branch of the Nile in Ethiopia.

Savannah
The southern countries of East Africa contain large areas of savannah, or grassland scattered with acacia and baobab trees. This region is home to much of Africa's wildlife, including antelopes, giraffes, and zebras, and their predators such as lions and hyenas.

Kilimanjaro
Africa's highest peak at 5,895 m (19,341 ft), the snow-capped Mount Kibo is one of the Kilimanjaro group of three volcanoes. The group dominates Arusha National Park in Tanzania, on the border with Kenya. Steam and fumes smoking from Kibo's crater indicate that the volcano is not yet extinct, adding to the attraction for mountaineers.

Regional climate
East Africa's climate is affected by altitude. Dominated by desert, Djibouti, and parts of Egypt, Eritrea, Ethiopia, Sudan, and Somalia are plagued by droughts. South Sudan and western Ethiopia receive seasonal rainfall, while parts of Tanzania, Kenya, and Uganda are hot and dry; their highlands are wet.

23°C (73°F) 20°C (68°F) 580 mm (23 in)

Nomadic herding
Many of the original peoples of eastern Africa, particularly the Dinka of Sudan, are nomads, who move from place to place with their herds of cattle in search of water and grazing land. However, competition for land is forcing many nomads to seek alternative lifestyles. Some men now take occasional work in cities or on construction sites.

Egypt

Today, as throughout its 5,000-year history, Egypt depends on the River Nile for much of its water, food, transport, and energy now generated at the massive Aswan Dam. Egypt controls the Suez Canal, an important shipping route that links Africa, Europe, and Asia, and brings money into the country. About 99 per cent of Egypt's people live along the lush, fertile banks of the river, and most are farmers, although the oil industry and tourist trade provide a growing number of jobs.

Water is drawn up to feed pipes that lead into the fields.

People

Several ethnic groups live in Egypt. Most people speak Arabic, but there are Berber and Nubian minorities. Until recently urban women were among the most liberated in the Arab world, but that may change with the rise of Islamic fundamentalism. In rural families, men go out to work, while women cook and fetch water.

EGYPT FACTS

CAPITAL CITY Cairo

AREA 1,001,450 sq km (386,660 sq miles)

POPULATION 69,100,000

DENSITY 69 people per sq km (154 per sq mile)

MAIN LANGUAGE Arabic

MAJOR RELIGION Muslim

CURRENCY Egyptian pound

LIFE EXPECTANCY 67 years

PEOPLE PER DOCTOR 625

GOVERNMENT Multi-party democracy

ADULT LITERACY 55%

A

Farming

Egypt is one of the world's leading producers of dates, which are mostly grown in oases, along with melons. While some farmers use modern methods, many *fellahin*, or peasant farmers, use centuries-old techniques such as this one, where the donkey drives a wheel that scoops up water for irrigation.

Food

Reputed to be as old as the Pyramids, the traditional Egyptian dish of *ful medames* is made by boiling broad beans with garlic, onion, olive oil, and spices. The beans are served with hard-boiled eggs, lemon, and unleavened bread. Food is often accompanied by sweet tea and coffee.

Ful medames

Tourism

Millions of people flock to Egypt every year to see the Pyramids and other remains of the country's ancient past, such as the tombs in the Valleys of the Kings and Queens, and the temples at Karnak and Luxor. The oldest pyramid is the Step Pyramid at Saqqara, which was built about 2650 BC as a tomb for King Zoser.

Ramesses II statue, Temple of Luxor

Soft dusters on poles are used to clean the delicate sandstone.

Cotton plant

Cairo

Egypt's ancient capital is the largest city in Africa, with a population of more than 7,000,000. It has at least 1,000 mosques, some built with stone looted from the Pyramids. Old Cairo's narrow streets heave with bustling bazaars, while the wealthy west bank has modern casinos and hotels.

The Sultan Hassan Mosque and surrounding area

Suez Canal

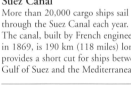

More than 20,000 cargo ships sail through the Suez Canal each year. The canal, built by French engineers in 1869, is 190 km (118 miles) long and provides a short cut for ships between the Gulf of Suez and the Mediterranean Sea.

Cotton

Although only five per cent of Egypt's land can be farmed, the country is a leading producer of cotton. Quality cloths are exported or made into cool garments like *jelebas*, or tunics, often worn by locals.

Cotton boll

Sudan

Sudan is the largest country in Africa, measuring 2,050 km (1,274 miles) long from north to south. Desert in the north gives way to a central, grassy plain. Marshland covers much of the south. Two branches of the Nile (the White Nile and the Blue Nile) meet at the capital, Khartoum, providing fertile soil for farming. The country has good oil and mineral resources, but war and drought have weakened it.

People

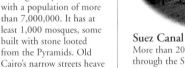

There are more than 500 Sudanese ethnic groups, speaking about 100 languages and dialects. Some are nomadic herders, many of whom have now settled on farms. Most own their own plots, and live in villages of mud huts along the Nile, where farming is combined with fishing. The produce is sold at markets. Civil war and famine in the south of Sudan have created refugees.

SUDAN FACTS

CAPITAL CITY Khartoum

AREA 2,505,810 sq km (967,493 sq miles)

POPULATION 31,800,000

MAIN LANGUAGE Arabic

MAJOR RELIGIONS Muslim, traditional beliefs, Christian

CURRENCY Sudanese pound or dinar

Religious conflict

The ruling people of the north are Arab Muslims, and the tall minarets of their beautiful mosques dominate the landscape. Farther south, the majority are divided into many ethnic groups and follow Christianity or traditional African religions. The religious, cultural, and language differences between north and south have caused bitter fighting.

Eritrea

A small, hot country on the Horn of Africa, Eritrea won independence from Ethiopia in 1993 after a 30-year war with Ethiopian troops, which left a legacy of destruction and further war. Vast, but as yet, unexploited copper resources around the rugged mountains have potential for development. Eritrea's strategic Red Sea coastal position gives it access to the sea's oil fields, fishing grounds, and useful trade routes.

ERITREA FACTS

CAPITAL CITY Asmara

AREA 121,320 sq km (46,842 sq miles)

POPULATION 3,800,000

MAIN LANGUAGES Tigrinya, Arabic

MAJOR RELIGIONS Christian, Muslim

CURRENCY Nakfa

Subsistence farming
More than 80 per cent of Eritreans live by subsistence farming, many of them as nomadic herders. Farmers depend on September rains to create seasonal rivers that water the harvest, but recurring droughts have meant that Eritrea has been forced to rely on food aid from overseas.

People
The long war of independence developed a strong sense of nationalism among the people, although they belong to several ethnic groups speaking different languages. Women, 30,000 of whom fought in the war, many at leadership level, have been pressing the government for equal rights in the country's new political constitution.

Somalia

An arid, flat country bordering the Indian Ocean, Somalia has some of the longest beaches in the world. The country gained independence in 1960, but since the late 1980s the south has been in the grip of civil war, waged by wealthy rival warlords, and has had no effective government. Most people are poor, and live in coastal towns in the north and in the south near rivers.

SOMALIA FACTS

CAPITAL CITY Mogadishu

AREA 637,657 sq km (246,199 sq miles)

POPULATION 9,200,000

MAIN LANGUAGES Somali, Arabic

MAJOR RELIGION Muslim

CURRENCY Somali shilling

Mogadishu
Conveniently situated on Somalia's coastline, Mogadishu has long been an important port. Arabs founded the capital more than 1,000 years ago, and sold it to the Italians in 1905. In 1960, it was returned to Somalia. The city's buildings are a mixture of older Arab architecture and 20th-century Italian design, but many have been damaged by war.

Civil war
Traditionally, the Somalis were organized in clans, or loyal family groups, that were controlled by elder members. The government destroyed the clan system in the 1980s, provoking bitter wars. Many people are now dependent on overseas aid.

Ethiopia

The Great Rift Valley, a high plateau, and an arid desert dominate Ethiopia. The country has suffered famine, drought, and civil war, but farming reforms and good seasonal rains have enabled Ethiopians to depend less on aid from abroad. Four-fifths of the population make their living through farming. Unique traditions like storytelling, music, and dance are an important part of everyday life.

ETHIOPIA FACTS

CAPITAL CITY Addis Ababa

AREA 1,127,127 sq km (435,184 sq miles)

POPULATION 64,500,000

MAIN LANGUAGE Amharic

MAJOR RELIGIONS Muslim, Christian, traditional beliefs

CURRENCY Ethiopian Birr

Vegetable dish made from cabbage, carrots, garlic, and red lentils

Hard-boiled egg

Chicken stew with egg, and red peppers

Enjera

A stew of beef, cinnamon, peppers, red chilli, and tomatoes

Red onions, chillies, garlic, and ginger, make wat, *a spicy sauce.*

Food
Spicy foods are standard in Ethiopia. A hot sauce, known as *wat*, is served with beef or chicken, and mopped up with bread. Usually, a soft, flat bread called *enjera* is eaten, which is made from teff, a field crop grown mainly in Ethiopia. A wide range of fish is available to those with money. Ethiopian *kaffa*, coffee flavoured with rye, is known as "health of Adam".

Orthodox priests

Orthodox Church
The Ethiopian Orthodox Church is the chief Christian faith in the country. The pilgrimage centre of Lalibela, in Ethiopia's central highlands, is known for its Christian churches, which date from the 10th century. *Timkat*, a yearly festival, is celebrated by many Ethiopian Christians.

Djibouti

A desert country on the Gulf of Aden, Djibouti serves as a port for Ethiopia. The two ethnic groups, the Afars and Issas, have a tradition of nomadic herding, but now half of them live in settled homes in the capital, Djibouti.

DJIBOUTI FACTS

CAPITAL CITY Djibouti

AREA 22,000 sq km (8,494 sq miles)

POPULATION 644,000

MAIN LANGUAGES Arabic, French

MAJOR RELIGIONS Muslim, Christian

CURRENCY Djibouti Franc

Shipping and fishing
The 19th-century city of Djibouti is one of the key Red Sea ports in the area, and generates much of the country's income. The fishing industry thrives on its rich waters.

Kenya

Lying on the Equator, Kenya has a varied landscape. The arid north is hot, but there is a rich farming region along the coast, and the southwestern highlands are warm and wet. The country has a stable, prosperous economy based on agriculture. More than 90 per cent of the Kenyan people are under the age of 45 and belong to about 70 ethnic groups. Kenya is noted for its wildlife and its spectacular national parks.

KENYA FACTS

CAPITAL CITY	Nairobi
AREA	582,650 sq km (224,961 sq miles)
POPULATION	31,300,000
MAIN LANGUAGES	Kiswahili, English
MAJOR RELIGIONS	Christian, traditional beliefs, Muslim
CURRENCY	Kenya shilling

A

Nairobi
Founded by British colonists as a railway town in 1899, Nairobi is Kenya's capital and a centre of business and communications. Home to 2,564,500 people, the city's high-rise buildings contrast with the surrounding plains where elephants and lions roam.

Tourism
National parks are the main attraction for the thousands of tourists who visit Kenya every year. Ten per cent of all Kenya is designated parkland, and there are more than 40 major national reserves. Amboseli, where many African animals (including lions, antelopes, and leopards) live, enjoys a spectacular view of Kilimanjaro.

Coffee beans

Tea leaves

Green beans

Crops
About 85 per cent of the population work on the land. Kenya is the world's fourth largest producer of tea, which, together with coffee, is grown on plantations. Kenya leads the world in the export of pyrethrum, a pink flower that is dried to make insecticides.

Uganda

Independence from Britain in 1962 led to ethnic conflict and poverty in Uganda, but since 1986, when peace was restored, the economy has been recovering slowly. Agriculture is still the main activity, with coffee, cotton, and cane sugar the main exports. Uganda also has good mineral deposits, including copper, gold, and cobalt. Most Ugandans live in rural villages.

UGANDA FACTS

CAPITAL CITY	Kampala
AREA	236,040 sq km (91,135 sq miles)
POPULATION	24,000,000
MAIN LANGUAGES	English, Kiswahili
MAJOR RELIGIONS	Christian, traditional beliefs, Muslim
CURRENCY	New Uganda shilling

Sweet potatoes

Market in Kampala

Farming
About 80 per cent of the work-force farm 43 per cent of the land. Most people own small farms, producing enough cassava, maize, millet, and sweet potatoes for themselves and to trade at market.

Kampala
Uganda's capital, Kampala, stands on hills overlooking Lake Victoria. The ancient palace of the former Buganda kings stands alongside the modern Makerere University. The 953,400 people of Kampala experience violent thunderstorms on an average of 242 days a year, and rain nearly every day.

Lake Victoria
The world's second largest freshwater lake, Victoria lies between Uganda, Kenya, and Tanzania. Giant perch fish have eaten nearly all the lake's natural fish species. A hydroelectricity project at the lake's Owen Falls aims to cut Uganda's oil imports in half.

Tanzania

The islands of Zanzibar united with mainland Tanganyika in 1964, creating Tanzania. More than half the country is covered by forests, and it has a long Indian Ocean coastline. Dar es Salaam, the largest city and chief port, was until recently the capital. Farming is the main activity, but oil, diamonds, and gas have been discovered.

TANZANIA FACTS

CAPITAL CITY	Dodoma
AREA	945,087 sq km (364,898 sq miles)
POPULATION	36,000,000
MAIN LANGUAGES	English, Kiswahili
MAJOR RELIGIONS	Traditional beliefs, Muslim, Christian
CURRENCY	Tanzania shilling

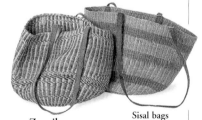

Cotton
Tea, tobacco, and cotton account for two-thirds of Tanzania's exports. Most cotton is produced on government-operated farms in the north and south highlands and around Lake Victoria. Workers carry the cotton to the factory to be spun and woven into cloth.

Sisal bags

People
The 120 ethnic groups of Tanzania live together in harmony, as no single group is dominant. More than two thirds of the people live in small, scattered villages, but the state *Ujamaa* policy has tried to resettle them into larger communities to provide more facilities.

Zanzibar
The island of Zanzibar and its small companion island of Pemba lie off the east coast of Tanzania. Zanzibar is one of the world's leading producers of cloves and sisal, a plant grown for making rope and bags for export.

FIND OUT MORE

AFRICA, HISTORY OF   CHRISTIANITY   DAMS   EGYPT, ANCIENT   EMPIRES   FARMING   ISLAM   PORTS AND WATERWAYS   RIVERS   WARFARE

AFRICA, NORTHWEST

MOROCCO, ALGERIA, TUNISIA, and Libya, plus the disputed territory of Western Sahara, make up the northwest corner of Africa. The region has been dominated by Arabs and their religion, Islam, for more than 1,300 years. Algeria and Libya are huge countries, but much of the land is desert. However, they and Tunisia have abundant reserves of oil and natural gas. Farming, made possible by irrigation projects, is still important to the region. Many people lead nomadic lives roaming the land with their herds of animals.

Mediterranean coast
Once occupied by the Phoenicians, Greeks, and Romans, northwest Africa's Mediterranean coast has many ancient ruins that are particularly popular with tourists in Morocco, Algeria, and Tunisia. Most people live on the coastal plain, which has fertile land and a warm climate.

Physical features

Along the Mediterranean and Atlantic coasts is a fertile strip where most of the people live. The Atlas Mountain chain runs across Morocco and continues as rolling hills in Algeria and Tunisia. The rest of the land is desert, broken by oases and bleak mountain ranges.

Atlas Mountains
The Atlas Mountains consist of several chains of mountains that stretch 2,410 km (1,500 miles) from the Atlantic coast of Morocco to Cape Bon in eastern Tunisia. The highest peak is Djebel Toubkal at 4,167 m (13,665 ft), which lies in the High Atlas range in southern Morocco.

25°C (77°F)   12°C (-53°F)

434 mm (17 in)

Regional climate
Along most of the coast and on high ground, summers are hot and dry and winters are warm and wet. Daytime desert temperatures average about 38°C (100°F); at night they are low. Desert rainfall may be as little as 2.5 cm (1 in) a year, and irregular.

Sahara
The Sahara Desert covers about 9,065,000 sq km (3,263,400 sq miles). Only about one-fifth is sand. The rest includes vast, flat expanses of barren rock and gravel and mountains such as Algeria's Ahaggar range, peaking at 2,918 m (9,573 ft). Crops are grown in 90 large oases.

Berbers

The original people of Northwest Africa are the Berbers. Today, about 15,000,000 Berbers still live in the mountains and deserts of the region. Most are Muslim, but retain their own language and dialects. The Tuareg are a group of nomadic Berber herders who roam the North African desert.

Berber man and child

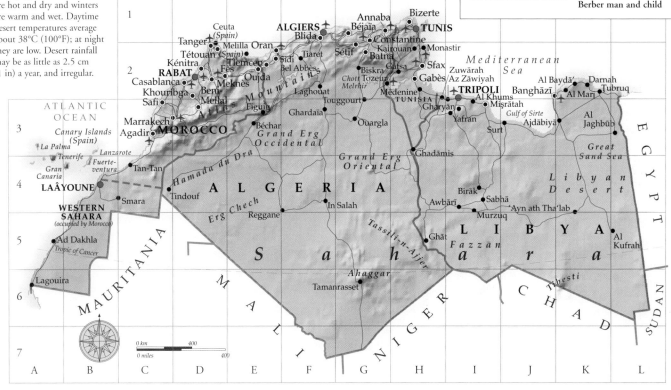

Morocco

A mix of African, Islamic, Arab, Berber, and European influences, Morocco attracts more than four million tourists each year. The country's strengths are farming and phosphate mining. Founded in Fès, in AD 859, Karueein University is the oldest in the world.

MOROCCO FACTS

CAPITAL CITY	Rabat
AREA	446,300 sq km (172,316 sq miles)
POPULATION	30,400,000
MAIN LANGUAGES	Arabic, Berber, French
MAJOR RELIGION	Muslim
CURRENCY	Moroccan dirham

Mint tea

The traditional drink in Morocco is a refreshing mint tea, served in glasses or pots, with plenty of sugar and a sprig of mint. It is often offered free of charge in the *souks* (markets), when bargaining is about to begin.

Carpets

Hand-knotted woollen carpets are one of Morocco's great craft industries. The leading carpet factories are in Fès and Rabat. The carpets have bold colours and symbolic, abstract Islamic patterns. Though sold by men, most rugs are made by women.

Polisario soldiers keep watch

Western Sahara

Morocco has occupied the ex-Spanish colony of Western Sahara since 1975. Polisario Front guerrillas began fighting for independence in 1983, to resist mass settlement of the area by Moroccans keen to hold on to the phosphate-rich territory.

Tunisia

A former French colony, Tunisia is the smallest country in the region and one of the more liberal Arab states. Although not admitted into politics, Tunisian women enjoy a high level of equality, making up 31 per cent of the work-force.

TUNISIA FACTS

CAPITAL CITY	Tunis
AREA	163,610 sq km (63,169 sq miles)
POPULATION	9,600,000
MAIN LANGUAGES	Arabic, French
MAJOR RELIGION	Muslim
CURRENCY	Tunisian dinar

Couscous is steamed in a special pot that sits above the stewing meat.

Couscous

The staple food in Tunisia is granules of semolina called couscous. Originally a Berber dish, couscous is served with a meat or vegetable sauce. Tunisians like their food spicy. After this main course, dates stuffed with almond paste, or sweet pastries filled with honey and nuts are served.

Souk

A feature of Tunisian cities – and indeed all northwest African cities – is the *souk*, or market. This is traditionally a tangle of narrow streets flanked by open-fronted stalls, where people can buy anything from food to carpets or hand-made jewellery.

Algeria

Under French rule from 1830, Algeria won independence in 1962. The country has a high birth rate and a young population: 86 per cent are below the age of 44. Crude oil and natural gas are an important source of income. Increasingly, fundamentalist Islamic groups pose a threat to non-Muslims.

ALGERIA FACTS

CAPITAL CITY	Algiers
AREA	2,381,740 sq km (919,590 sq miles)
POPULATION	30,800,000
MAIN LANGUAGES	Arabic, Berber, French, Tamazight
MAJOR RELIGION	Muslim
CURRENCY	Algerian dinar

Overpopulation

Since more than four-fifths of Algeria is desert, 90 per cent of Algerians live in the far north of the country, where it is cooler. However, as Algeria's population continues to increase at a rate of more than 1.7 per cent a year, many northern towns, like Constantine, are struggling to house everybody, and slum areas are growing.

Houses are built on every available piece of land.

Black dates

Yellow dates

Dates

Algeria is the world's sixth largest producer of dates. They are grown in the fertile north as well as in the many oases of the Sahara, and provide a main source of income. Date palms also yield timber; their leaves are used to thatch buildings.

Libya

Since 95 per cent of Libya is desert, the Great Man-made River Project was set up to irrigate farming land. Water is piped from beneath the Sahara to populated coastal regions.

LIBYA FACTS

CAPITAL CITY	Tripoli
AREA	1,759,540 sq km (679, 358 sq miles)
POPULATION	5,400,000
MAIN LANGUAGES	Arabic, Tuareg
MAJOR RELIGION	Muslim
CURRENCY	Libyan dinar

Oil and gas

The discovery of oil and natural gas in 1959 transformed Libya into a wealthy nation, and many people moved to the towns in search of work. In 1992, trade with the West was severely disrupted when the UN imposed sanctions because of Libya's alleged links with terrorist groups. These sanctions were lifted in 2003.

Oil workers at Calanscio

Roman ruins

Libya was abandoned by the Romans after the Arab conquest of AD 643 and was an Italian colony between 1911 and 1951. Today, some of the finest Roman ruins outside Italy can be seen at Leptis Magna, now called Labdah, to the east of the capital, Tripoli.

FIND OUT MORE · AFRICA, HISTORY OF · DESERTS · EMPIRES · FARMING · ISLAM · ISLAMIC EMPIRE · MOUNTAINS AND VALLEYS · OIL · ROMAN EMPIRE · TEXTILES AND WEAVING

AFRICA, SOUTHERN CENTRAL

SOUTHERN CENTRAL AFRICA is made up of
seven countries that form part of the African
mainland, and the islands of Madagascar
and Comoros in the Indian Ocean. Farming
is still an important source of income in these countries, but
major deposits of minerals such as diamonds, copper, uranium,
and iron have led many people to move to the towns and cities
in search of work. A variety of tribal groups, each with its own
language, customs, and beliefs, lives in
the southern central region.

Namib Desert
The Namib Desert extends 1,900 km (1,100 miles)
in a narrow strip from southwestern Angola, along the
Skeleton Coast of Namibia, and down to the border of
South Africa. Although it rarely rains, the climate on
the coast is humid with cold, morning fogs. Sand
dunes reach down to the edge of the Atlantic and
the only practical means of transport is the camel.

Physical features

Although lowlands fringe the coast, most of
the region lies 400–1,500 m (1,200–4,500 ft)
above sea-level. The landscape includes the
Namib and Kalahari deserts in the west and
centre, dry savannah and woodland, and
humid, subtropical forests in the north.

Acacia trees,
Madagascar

Savannah
Much of the region is covered by grassland, or
savannah. The most common trees in these areas
are thorn trees, especially acacias. They are suited
to the dry conditions and grow on the edges of the
Kalahari and other
semi-desert regions.

Regional climate
Most of the region lies in the tropics, where the climate
is always hot, but there are two seasons: wet and dry. Rain
is heavy in the wet season. Most of Botswana and Namibia
has a semi-arid climate, and much of Namibia is desert.
Eastern Madagascar has a tropical wet climate.

23°C
(74°F)   16°C
(61°F)

964 mm
(38 in)

Women's role
The traditional role of African women
was to look after the home and bring up
the children. Many were also expected to
cultivate the crops, and some built their
own houses. Today, many women in
southern central Africa have additional
responsibilities, because their husbands
are away working in mines and cities.
Despite the domestic power of women,
few have official jobs or own property.

Zimbabwean
woman with
her baby

Angola

In 1975, after a long war, Angola became independent of Portuguese colonial rule. With fertile land and huge reserves of diamonds, oil, and natural gas, the country should have become prosperous. However, Angola was torn apart and economic development was restricted by the fighting that continued after independence. Civil war erupted between rival ethnic groups and continues today.

ANGOLA FACTS

CAPITAL CITY Luanda

AREA 1,246,700 sq km (481,351 sq miles)

POPULATION 13,500,000

MAIN LANGUAGE Portuguese

MAJOR RELIGIONS Christian, traditional beliefs

CURRENCY Readjusted kwanza

Oil and diamonds
Most of Angola's oil is produced in Cabinda, a tiny Angolan enclave in Dem. Rep. Congo. Petroleum provides 90 per cent of Angola's exports. Angola also ranks highly in world output of diamonds, its second largest export.

Luanda
Founded by the Portuguese in 1575, Angola's capital and largest city is home to more than 2,500,000 people. Once used for shipping slaves to Brazil, it is still a major seaport. Modern Luanda is an industrial centre with its own oil refinery.

Zambia

Bordered to the south by the Zambezi River, Zambia is a country of upland plateaus, 80 per cent of which are grassland and forest. About 50 per cent of the people live by subsistence farming, constantly threatened by drought. Tobacco is the main exported crop. Hydroelectric power provides much of Zambia's energy. Low copper prices in the 1980s upset finances.

ZAMBIA FACTS

CAPITAL CITY Lusaka

AREA 752,614 sq km (290,584 sq miles)

POPULATION 10,600,000

MAIN LANGUAGES English, Bemba, Tonga, Nyanja, Lozi, Lunda

MAJOR RELIGIONS Christian, traditional beliefs

CURRENCY Zambian kwacha

Cobalt is used in steel production.

Copper forms 90 per cent of exports.

Copper bracelets

Copper and cobalt
Zambia is the world's sixth largest producer of copper. The seam of copper ore where the metal is mined, the Copperbelt, is 320 km (200 miles) long. The second largest producer of cobalt, Zambia also mines lead, silver, and zinc.

Urban living
About half of Zambia's people, a mix of more than 70 different ethnic groups, live in towns and cities. The most populated area is the Copperbelt, where most of them work. The capital, Lusaka, a thriving industrial and business centre, is home to 1,800,000 Zambians.

Namibia

An ex-German colony, and ruled for 70 years by South Africa, Namibia won its independence in 1990. Rich mineral resources make mining the country's leading industry. One in seven people lives on the land, mainly rearing livestock, although drought and the expanding desert make farming difficult. Fishing is good off the Atlantic coast.

NAMIBIA FACTS

CAPITAL CITY Windhoek

AREA 825,418 sq km (318,694 sq miles)

POPULATION 1,800,000

MAIN LANGUAGES English, Afrikaans, Ovambo, Kavango

MAJOR RELIGION Christian

CURRENCY Namibian dollar

Uranium
The Rössing Uranium Mine in the Namib Desert is the world's largest, producing 2,000 tonnes (2,200 tons) of uranium every year. Namibia is the world's fifth largest producer of uranium and ranks among the top producers of diamonds.

People
Namibia has a peaceful multiracial society. The white minority lives mostly in Windhoek, in European-style houses. Black Namibians include many groups, the largest of which are the northern Ovambo. To the west, the semi-nomadic Himba raise cattle.

Himba woman

Hair is braided and beaded.

Botswana

Southwest Botswana is covered by the Kalahari Desert. To the north is the marshy delta of the Okavango River, a haven for wildlife. Despite this wetland, however, Botswana suffers droughts. Most people live in the more fertile east. Production of diamonds – the third largest in the world – has helped to stimulate Botswana's economy.

BOTSWANA FACTS

CAPITAL CITY Gaborone

AREA 600,370 sq km (231,803 sq miles)

POPULATION 1,600,000

MAIN LANGUAGES English, Tswana, Shona, Khoikhoi, Ndebele

MAJOR RELIGIONS Traditional beliefs, Christian

CURRENCY Pula

San
The original inhabitants of Botswana are the nomadic San people, once known as Kalahari Bushmen, one of Africa's only remaining groups of hunter-gatherers. There are fewer than 50,000 San today, but small groups still roam the Kalahari Desert hunting small animals and eating edible plants and insects. Many San now work on cattle ranches.

Beef stew with dried spinach

Savoury porridge

Food
The Tswana people, who make up the majority of Botswana's population, live mostly by subsistence farming, raising cattle, and growing enough maize, sorghum, and millet for their own use. Their staple diet consists of meat stews served with a kind of porridge made from cereals. Fresh vegetables are rare.

A

Zimbabwe

In 1980, the former British colony of Rhodesia became independent and took the name Zimbabwe, after the ancient city of Great Zimbabwe. About 70 per cent of Zimbabweans live from farming. Coal, gold, asbestos, and nickel are mined for export. Zimbabwe has recently suffered great disruption over the issues of government and land re-distribution.

ZIMBABWE FACTS

CAPITAL CITY Harare

AREA 390,580 sq km (150,803 sq miles)

POPULATION 12,900,000

MAIN LANGUAGES English, Shona, Ndebele

MAJOR RELIGIONS Traditional beliefs, Christian

CURRENCY Zimbabwe dollar

Tourism
Zimbabwe's main tourist attractions are the spectacular Victoria Falls, the Kariba Dam, national parks, and the ruins of the city of Great Zimbabwe. Tourists enjoy action holidays, such as canoeing and rafting, on the Zambezi.

Harare
Formerly called Salisbury, the capital is Zimbabwe's commercial and industrial centre and home to almost two million people. It is a clean and sophisticated city that is characterized by flowering trees, colourful parks, and modern buildings.

Madagascar

The fourth largest island in the world, Madagascar is home to some unique wildlife because of its isolated position off Africa's east coast. A high plateau runs the length of the island, dropping to a narrow, fertile strip in the east, where most people live. The country's economy is based on growing crops and raising livestock.

MADAGASCAR FACTS

CAPITAL CITY Antananarivo

AREA 587,040 sq km (226,656 sq miles)

POPULATION 16,400,000

MAIN LANGUAGES Malagasy, French

MAJOR RELIGIONS Traditional beliefs, Christian, Muslim

CURRENCY Malagasy franc

Vanilla
Madagascar is the world's largest exporter of vanilla. The pods of the plants are used to flavour ice-cream and chocolate. Other important cash crops are cloves, sisal, cocoa, and butter beans.

Vanilla pods grow 25 cm (10 in) long.

Rural society
Most Madagascans are descended from Asians from Malaysia and Indonesia, who began to settle on the island almost 2,000 years ago. Later waves of mainland Africans intermixed to produce a uniquely multiracial society. Three-quarters of the Madagascan labour force works on the land growing subsistence crops, such as cassava and rice.

Mozambique

As a result of years of civil war, flooding, and drought, Mozambique is now one of the world's poorest countries, with a high birth rate. The land, though largely unexploited, is fertile and rich in minerals. The ports and railways provide a trade link for land-locked Swaziland, Malawi, and Zimbabwe.

Fishing
One of Mozambique's key industries is fishing, and shrimps account for more than 40 per cent of export earnings. The country's total annual fish catch averages 24,170 tonnes (26,643 tons). Other exports include cotton, tea, and sugar.

MOZAMBIQUE FACTS

CAPITAL CITY Maputo

AREA 801,590 sq km (309,494 sq miles)

POPULATION 18,600,000

MAIN LANGUAGE Portuguese

MAJOR RELIGIONS Traditional beliefs, Christian, Muslim

CURRENCY Metical

Malawi

With few natural resources, Malawi has a rural society, despite the constant threat of drought. Light industries, such as food processing, textiles, and manufacturing farm tools, are developing. Fish from Lake Malawi, which covers one-quarter of the country, is a source of food.

MALAWI FACTS

CAPITAL CITY Lilongwe

AREA 118,480 sq km (45,745 sq miles)

POPULATION 11,600,000

MAIN LANGUAGES Chewa, English

MAJOR RELIGIONS Christian, Muslim

CURRENCY Malawian kwacha

Tea grows well in the tropical climate of Malawi's hillsides.

Farming
Almost 86 per cent of the Malawi labour force works in agriculture, growing cash crops, such as tea, tobacco, coffee, cotton, and sugar, as well as subsistence crops of maize, rice, cassava, and plantains. The country is self-sufficient in food.

Comoros

The three islands and few islets of the Comoros archipelago lie north of Madagascar in the Indian Ocean. They were governed by France until 1975. The economy is underdeveloped, and most of the people live by subsistence farming.

COMOROS FACTS

CAPITAL CITY Moroni

AREA 2,170 sq km (838 sq miles)

POPULATION 707,000

MAIN LANGUAGES Arabic, French, Comoran, local languages

MAJOR RELIGIONS Muslim

CURRENCY Comoros franc

Ylang-ylang
Comoros is the world's largest grower of ylang-ylang, an aromatic tree with greenish-yellow flowers that produce a pleasantly scented oil used to make perfume.

FIND OUT MORE   **AFRICA, HISTORY OF**   **AFRICAN WILDLIFE**   **DESERTS**   **EMPIRES**   **FARMING**   **FISHING INDUSTRY**   **GREAT ZIMBABWE**   **OIL**   **ROCKS AND MINERALS**   **SOCIETIES, HUMAN**

AFRICA, WEST

THE ATLANTIC OCEAN borders all but three of the 15 countries that make up West Africa. Much of the area is dominated by the Sahara and the Sahel, a vast area of semi-desert, which the Sahara is slowly invading. Despite their potential wealth and rich resources, most of the countries are desperately poor. Long-established trade routes across the Sahara link West Africa with the Mediterranean coast to the north. For millions of West Africans, life is a perpetual struggle against a hostile climate, the threat of drought, and political instability.

Sahel
Immediately south of the Sahara Desert, stretching all the way across West Africa, is a broad band of hot, arid, semi-desert grassland called the Sahel. In Arabic, the word Sahel means "shore" of the desert. Rainfall in this region is sporadic and droughts are common.

Regional climate   25°C (78°F)   26°C (80°F)
Moving from north to south, there are four main climate regions in West Africa: desert, Sahel, grassland, and tropical rainforest. Rain is rare in the northern desert and Sahel regions, yet the south is humid and tropical with a distinct rainy season that can last for four to six months.
1,879 mm (74 in)

Physical features

Most of West Africa lies 200–400 m (600–1200 ft) above sea-level. The Sahara dominates Niger, Mauritania, and Mali, and the Sahel extends south into Senegal, Burkina Faso, and Nigeria. The rivers Senegal, Gambia, Volta, and Niger irrigate the west and south.

River Niger
Africa's third longest river, the Niger flows in a great arc for 4,180 km (2,597 miles) from Guinea through Mali, Niger, Benin, and Nigeria to a vast delta on the Gulf of Guinea. A valuable source of fish and water, it is navigable for more than half its length.

Groundnuts
Also called peanuts, groundnuts develop underground. They are widely grown in West Africa as a source of edible oil, and as a foodstuff that is rich in protein and vitamins. The plants were introduced into West Africa from South America.

Harvesting peanuts

Mauritania

The northern two-thirds of Mauritania are desert. The only farmland lies in a narrow, fertile strip along the bank of the River Senegal in the southwest. This area is scattered with small villages and oases. Nomadic Moors of Arab descent, from the north, live in Mauritania. They have often clashed with black farmers in the south.

Fishing
The waters off Mauritania are said to have the richest fish stocks in the world; they attract many foreign fishing fleets. All catches must be sold through the state fishing company. Fishing provides more than half of Mauritania's export earnings.

Desertification
Successive years of drought and overgrazing in the Sahel region have caused the desert to expand southwards, killing livestock and forcing many nomads to move into towns.

Government schemes are attempting to reclaim the land by reducing soil erosion.

Mineral wealth
The Mauritanian desert contains the largest deposits of gypsum – used for making plaster – and some of the largest reserves of iron ore in the world. The country also exports gold. A single rail line connects mines with Nouakchott, the country's capital and main port.

Gypsum crystal

MAURITANIA FACTS

CAPITAL CITY	Nouakchott
AREA	1,030,700 sq km (397,953 sq miles)
POPULATION	2,700,000
MAIN LANGUAGES	Arabic, French, Hassaniya, Wolof, Soninké
MAJOR RELIGION	Muslim
CURRENCY	Ouguiya

Senegal

The flat, semi-desert plains of Senegal are crossed by four rivers – the Senegal, Gambia, Saloum, and Casamance – which provide water for agriculture, the country's main source of income. Tourism is also developing. Senegal has a mix of ethnic groups, the largest of which are the Wolofs.

Music
At festivals and ceremonies, or *griots*, a mix of historians, musicians, and poets, sing and recite traditional stories, often to the accompaniment of a *kora*.

Kora

Musicians pluck the 21 strings to give a wide range of muted sounds.

Many of Senegal's fruits and vegetables are imported and expensive.

Gourd soundbox

Dakar
Senegal's capital and major port, Dakar is a bustling industrial centre with good restaurants, shops, and markets. However, many of the 2,500,000 people who live here are poor and live in suburban slums.

SENEGAL FACTS

CAPITAL CITY	Dakar
AREA	196,190 sq km (75,749 sq miles)
POPULATION	9,700,000
MAIN LANGUAGES	French, Wolof, Fulani, Sérèr, Diola, Mandinka
MAJOR RELIGIONS	Muslim, Christian, traditional beliefs
CURRENCY	CFA franc

Farming
About 60 per cent of the Senegalese labour force works on the land growing cotton and sugar-cane for export, and rice, sorghum, and millet for their food. Until droughts in the 1970s damaged yields, groundnuts were the main cash crop. Fish is now the main export.

Gambia

One of the most densely populated countries in Africa, Gambia occupies a narrow strip either side of the River Gambia and is surrounded on three sides by Senegal. With little industry, 80 per cent of the people live off the land. Groundnuts make up 80 per cent of exports. The main ethnic groups are the Mandingo, Fulani, and Wolof.

GAMBIA FACTS

CAPITAL CITY	Banjul
AREA	11,300 sq km (4,363 sq miles)
POPULATION	1,340,000
MAIN LANGUAGES	English, Mandinka
MAJOR RELIGIONS	Muslim, Christian, traditional beliefs
CURRENCY	Dalasi

Tourism
Gambia is an attractive destination for winter sun-seekers from Europe. Tourism, the country's fastest-growing industry, employs one in ten Gambians. About 10,000 of those work on a seasonal basis.

Guinea-Bissau

Rainfall in Guinea-Bissau is more reliable than in most of the rest of Africa, enabling the country to be self-sufficient in rice. However, flooding is common along the coast because farmers have cut down mangroves to plant rice fields. Most people travel by boat.

Cashew nuts

Grated coconut

Coconut

GUINEA-BISSAU FACTS

CAPITAL CITY	Bissau
AREA	36,120 sq km (13,946 sq miles)
POPULATION	1,200,000
MAIN LANGUAGES	Portuguese, Crioulo
MAJOR RELIGIONS	Traditional beliefs, Muslim, Christian
CURRENCY	CFA Franc

Cashew nuts
Farming employs 85 per cent of the work-force. Rice, cotton, groundnuts, and copra are produced as cash crops, as are cashew nuts, which make up nearly 60 per cent of the country's exports.

A

Guinea

With more than 30 per cent of the world's known reserves of bauxite, and deposits of diamonds, iron, copper, manganese, uranium and gold, Guinea could be a wealthy country. However, years of poor government and lack of support from former French rulers have made Guinea's economic development difficult.

GUINEA FACTS

CAPITAL CITY Conakry

AREA 245,857 sq km (94,925 sq miles)

POPULATION 8,300,000

MAIN LANGUAGES French, Fulani, Malinke, Susu

MAJOR RELIGIONS Muslim, traditional beliefs, Christian

CURRENCY Guinea franc

Coffee beans

Bananas

Pineapple

Fruit growing
Bananas, plantains, and pineapples grow well in the fertile Fouta Djalon hills (Guinea Highlands). Farmers cultivate coffee, palm nuts, and groundnuts as cash crops and sorghum, rice, and cassava for their families.

People
Three-quarters of Guineans belong to one of three main ethnic groups – the Malinke and Fulani who live in the north and centre, and the Susu who live closer to the coast. Two-thirds live in small rural communities, where the standard of living is one of the lowest in the world. Average life expectancy is low, at only 45 years, and only about 35 per cent of people can read.

Sierra Leone

Sierra Leone was founded by the British in the early 1800s as a colony for freed slaves. Its name is Spanish for "Lion Mountains" and refers to the constant roar of thunder. Of the 12 ethnic groups, the biggest are the Mende and the Temne. A ceasefire halted civil war in 2000.

SIERRA LEONE FACTS

CAPITAL CITY Freetown

AREA 71,740 sq km (27,698 sq miles)

POPULATION 4,600,000

MAIN LANGUAGES English, Krio (Creole)

MAJOR RELIGIONS Traditional beliefs, Muslim, Christian

CURRENCY Leone

Industry
Mining is the mainstay of Sierra Leone's economy. The chief exports are diamonds, some of which are still mined by hand, as well as gold, bauxite, and titanium ore. Farming employs more than two-thirds of the work-force, growing coffee, cocoa, palm kernels, ginger, and cassava.

Uncut diamond looks like any other stone.

Freetown
Surrounded by green hills, Sierra Leone's capital, Freetown, is a colourful and historic port and home to more than 700,000 people. The name is a reminder of the country's former status as a haven for freed slaves. Among Freetown's attractions are a 500-year-old cotton tree, and West Africa's oldest university, built in 1827.

Ivory Coast

With 600 km (370 miles) of Atlantic coastline, and three main rivers, Ivory Coast is fertile and farming efficient. It is among the world's top producers of coffee and cocoa. Food accounts for half of all exports. Most people work in farming and forestry. Nearly all the forests have been sold off as timber to pay foreign debts.

IVORY COAST FACTS

CAPITAL CITY Yamoussoukro

AREA 322,460 sq km (124,502 sq miles)

POPULATION 16,300,000

MAIN LANGUAGES French, Akan

MAJOR RELIGIONS Muslim, Christian, traditional beliefs

CURRENCY CFA franc

Farmers use pesticides on cocoa plantations, but the lack of protective clothes is a serious health risk.

Yamoussoukro Basilica
Although only 29 per cent of the people of the population are Christian, Ivory Coast has one of the world's largest Christian churches. Able to seat 7,000 people, it dominates the city of Yamoussoukro, which replaced Abidjan as the country's capital in 1983.

Cocoa
Ivory Coast is the world's leading producer of cocoa beans. Cocoa trees need humid conditions, and many cocoa plantations lie in moist, tropical regions where rainforests were felled for timber. Factories have been set up in Ivory Coast to make cocoa butter, which is the basic ingredient of chocolate and some cosmetics.

Liberia

Founded by the USA in the 1820s as a home for freed black slaves, Liberia has never been colonized. About five per cent of the people descend from former slaves and American settlers. The rest are a varied mix of ethnic groups. About 70 per cent of Liberians work on the land, growing oil palms, coffee, and cocoa, and rubber for export. Civil war has damaged trade.

LIBERIA FACTS

CAPITAL CITY Monrovia

AREA 111,370 sq km (43,000 sq miles)

POPULATION 3,100,000

MAIN LANGUAGES English, Kpelle, Bassa, Vai, Grebo, Kru, Kissi, Gola

MAJOR RELIGIONS Christian, traditional beliefs, Muslim

CURRENCY Liberian dollar

Civil war
Since 1990, Liberia has been torn by a chaotic and bloody civil war, and its once prosperous economy has collapsed. The war, which began as clashes between various ethnic groups, has made thousands of people homeless and many are forced to live in large refugee camps where food shortages are a part of everyday life.

Monrovia
Reputedly the world's wettest capital city, with more than 4,560 mm (183 in) of rain per year, Monrovia is a sprawling city and major port. Liberia has the world's largest commercial fleet of ships. Almost all are foreign owned, but registered in Monrovia, where taxes are low.

A

Mali

Desert and semi-desert cover the northern two-thirds of Mali, and only two per cent of the land can be cultivated. Most people live in the south, in farming settlements close to the rivers Niger and Senegal. Droughts, poor food, and an average life expectancy of only 51 years, make Mali one of the world's poorest countries. Some gold is mined, but cotton is the biggest export.

Buildings such as this granary are made from sand bricks.

MALI FACTS

CAPITAL CITY Bamako

AREA 1,240,000 sq km (478,764 sq miles)

POPULATION 11,700,000

MAIN LANGUAGES French, Bambara, Mande, Arabic, Fulani, Senufo, Soninke

MAJOR RELIGIONS Muslim, traditional beliefs

CURRENCY CFA franc

Making "mud cloth"

People

Mali's main peoples are the Bambara, Fulani, Tuareg, and Dogon, with smaller numbers of Songhai and Bozo. Bozo artists, mostly women, are noted for their "mud cloth", made by painting abstract designs on to rough cloth using differently coloured soils.

Tombouctou

Lying on the edge of the desert, Tombouctou is a city of sand still visited by camel caravans carrying salt from mines in the north for shipping up the River Niger to Mopti. This historic city is a centre of Islamic learning.

Burkina

Land-locked in the arid Sahel region and threatened by the Sahara, which is expanding southwards, Burkina (formerly Upper Volta) is one of West Africa's poorest and most overpopulated countries. Faced with droughts and lack of work, many young people are forced to leave to find jobs abroad.

BURKINA FACTS

CAPITAL CITY Ouagadougou

AREA 274,200 sq km (105,869 sq miles)

POPULATION 11,900,000

MAIN LANGUAGES French, Mossi, Mande, Fulani, Lobi, Bobo

MAJOR RELIGIONS Traditional beliefs, Muslim, Christian

CURRENCY CFA franc

Fulani children

Fulani

The Fulani are nomadic cattle herders who roam West Africa with their animals. In Burkina, where they number about 75,000, they are one of more than 60 ethnic groups. Fulani herders traditionally tend cattle for local farmers in exchange for sacks of rice.

Cotton

Burkina's most valuable cash crop is cotton, which brings in about 25 per cent of its export earnings. However, the country's farming is threatened by the mass emigration of young workers, who send money home to their families. The country has deposits of silver and manganese, and exports gold.

Ghana

Once called the "Gold Coast" by Europeans who found gold here 500 years ago, Ghana still has reserves of gold, which has recently replaced cocoa as the country's major source of income. The country is still one of the world's largest cocoa producers. Lake Volta, formed by a dam on the River Volta, is the world's largest artificial lake.

GHANA FACTS

CAPITAL CITY Accra

AREA 238,540 sq km (92,100 sq miles)

POPULATION 19,700,000

MAIN LANGUAGES English, Akan, Mossi, Ewe, Ga, Twi, Fanti, Gurma

MAJOR RELIGIONS Christian, traditional beliefs, Muslim

CURRENCY Cedi

Eseye (a kind of spinach)

Plantains

Food

A popular food in Ghana is *banku*, a mixture of maize dough and cassava. Ghanaians mix leaves of *eseye*, a type of spinach, with palm oil to make a sauce that is eaten with boiled fish or vegetables.

People

Family ties are strong in Ghana, and the extended family is important. About half of Ghanaians are Ashanti people whose ancestors developed one of the richest and most famous civilizations in Africa. Other groups include the Mole-Dagbani, Ewe, and Ga. About 38 per cent of the people live in cities and towns.

Ghanaian family

Togo

A long, narrow country, just 110 km (68 miles) at its widest point, Togo has a central forested plateau with savannah to the north and south. Nearly half the population is under 15 years of age, and few people are more than 45. Although most people are farmers, Togo's main export is phosphates, used for making fertilizers.

TOGO FACTS

CAPITAL CITY Lomé

AREA 56,785 sq km (21,924 sq miles)

POPULATION 4,700,000

MAIN LANGUAGES French, Kabye, Ewe

MAJOR RELIGIONS Traditional beliefs, Christian, Muslim

CURRENCY CFA franc

Farming

Togolese farmers produce cocoa, coffee, cotton, copra, and palm kernels mainly for export. New products include herbs, tomatoes, and sugar. For their own use, they grow millet, cassava, and maize. Fishing is important in coastal areas.

Maize

Market women

Although politics and formal employment remain the domain of men, many Togolese women work informally in part-time jobs. The Nana Benz, wealthy women traders so-called because they all seem to own Mercedes Benz cars, dominate Togo's markets and taxi businesses. Based in the market at Lomé, these formidable women fight hard for business and have a legendary capacity for haggling.

Nigeria

With large reserves of oil, natural gas, coal, iron ore, lead, tin, and zinc, and rich, fertile farmland, Nigeria looked set to prosper when it gained independence from Britain in 1960. However, the country's economy has experienced difficulty due to falling oil prices, ethnic conflicts, and corrupt government. After 16 years of military dictatorship, civilian rule was restored in 1999.

Abuja

Begun in 1980, the new, purpose-built city of Abuja replaced Lagos as Nigeria's capital in 1991, because the government believed Lagos was too influenced by the Yoruba people. By the late 1990s, much of Abuja was unfinished as money ran low during construction.

Central mosque, Abuja

People

Nigerian society consists of an uneasy mix of more than 250 ethnic groups. Two-thirds of the population belongs to one of three groups – the Hausa in the north, the Ibo in the east, and the Yoruba in the west. About 57 per cent of people live in small tight-knit villages where communal life is important.

Nigerian oil has a low sulphur content and is ideal for aircraft fuel.

Oil

Nigeria's oil production, which ranks first in Africa and highly in the world, accounts for 95 per cent of all its exports. Almost totally dependent on this new industry, which began in the 1960s, Nigeria is vulnerable to changes in world oil prices.

Plantations

Agriculture employs more than 40 per cent of all Nigerian workers. Although most farmers work on small plots with simple tools, vast plantations have been established to cultivate cash crops on a commercial scale for export, using modern machinery. Crops include cotton, coffee, cocoa beans, and oil palms.

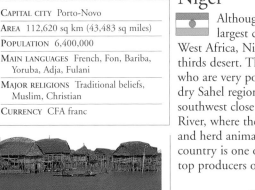

The best cloth is a mix of cotton and silk.

Cloth

Nigeria's Yoruba and Hausa peoples produce many attractive patterned textiles, hand-dyed using natural plant colours. In the Hausa town of Kano, in the north, men dye the cloth in ancient dye pits.

NIGERIA FACTS

CAPITAL CITY Abuja

AREA 923,768 sq km (356,667 sq miles)

POPULATION 116,900,000

DENSITY 128 per sq km (332 per sq mile)

MAIN LANGUAGES English, Hausa, Yoruba, Ibo

MAJOR RELIGIONS Muslim, Christian, traditional beliefs

CURRENCY Naira

LIFE EXPECTANCY 52 years

PEOPLE PER DOCTOR 5,000

GOVERNMENT Multiparty democracy

ADULT LITERACY 64%

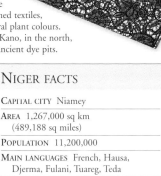

Benin

A former French colony, Benin took its name from an ancient empire, in 1975, 15 years after becoming independent. It is a long, narrow country with a short coastline on the Gulf of Guinea. Most of the land is flat and forested, with a large marsh in the south. Most people live off the land, producing yams, cassava, and maize. Cotton brings in about three-quarters of the country's export income.

BENIN FACTS

CAPITAL CITY Porto-Novo

AREA 112,620 sq km (43,483 sq miles)

POPULATION 6,400,000

MAIN LANGUAGES French, Fon, Bariba, Yoruba, Adja, Fulani

MAJOR RELIGIONS Traditional beliefs, Muslim, Christian

CURRENCY CFA franc

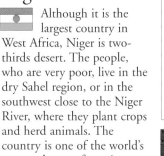

Fishing

Every year, fishermen catch about 39,000 tonnes (42,990 tons) of fish in the lagoons along the coast of Benin.

Betamaribé

One of five main ethnic groups in Benin, the Betamaribé, or Somba, live in the northwest near the Atakora Mountains. One of the first peoples to settle in Benin, they have lived free from Western influence for hundreds of years and have managed to keep many of their traditions intact.

Niger

Although it is the largest country in West Africa, Niger is two-thirds desert. The people, who are very poor, live in the dry Sahel region, or in the southwest close to the Niger River, where they plant crops and herd animals. The country is one of the world's top producers of uranium.

NIGER FACTS

CAPITAL CITY Niamey

AREA 1,267,000 sq km (489,188 sq miles)

POPULATION 11,200,000

MAIN LANGUAGES French, Hausa, Djerma, Fulani, Tuareg, Teda

MAJOR RELIGION Muslim

CURRENCY CFA franc

Fighting the desert

The people of Niger are waging a battle against the advance of the desert into the dry Sahel where they live. They plant trees and grass in an attempt to stop the soil eroding.

Male beauty contest

Every year, in a festival known as the *gerewol,* young Wodaabé men make themselves up to try and attract a wife in an unusual beauty contest. After much dancing, the women make their choice. If a marriage proposal results, the man kidnaps the woman, and they set off into the desert for a nomadic life together.

FIND OUT MORE | AFRICA, HISTORY OF | BENIN EMPIRE | CONSERVATION | DESERTS | FARMING | FISHING INDUSTRY | OIL | ROCKS AND MINERALS | SLAVERY | TEXTILES AND WEAVING

AFRICAN WILDLIFE

No OTHER CONTINENT matches the wealth of wildlife found in Africa. Covering the full climatic spectrum from intense heat to bitter cold, its varied vegetation has given rise to a wide range of animals, including mammals, birds, reptiles, fish, and insects. Among them are more than 40 species of primate, ranging from tiny galagos to huge gorillas, a great variety of antelopes, gazelles, and other hoofed animals, and 70 species of carnivore. Bird life, too, is extraordinarily rich; more than 1,500 species live south of the Sahara. In addition, Africa is inhabited by the world's fastest land animal, the cheetah; the biggest bird, the ostrich; and the largest land animal, the elephant.

Giraffe

The giraffe's great height – males reach up to 5.5 m (18 ft) – gives it the advantage of being able to spot danger from a distance and then escape at speed. It also enables the giraffe to browse on acacia leaves that are out of the reach of most other grassland animals, giving it a near monopoly of its principal food supply.

Patterned coat provides camouflage.

Long tail with coarse hair is used to deter flies.

Grassland wildlife

African grasslands (savannahs) sustain over 20 species of grazing animals, from the giant sable antelope to the tiny pygmy antelope. The herds of plains game and their predators, including lions, are pursued by scavengers such as hyenas and vultures. Grassland birds include the guineafowl and hornbills.

Long tail feathers help it balance when running.

Secretary bird

Among the most striking of Africa's grassland birds is the secretary bird, with its long legs and feathered crest. It rarely flies, preferring to walk, nodding its head with each step. It attacks snakes, spreading its wings over its body to shield itself from venomous bites, while using its feet to stamp them to death.

Long legs for running through grass after snakes and frogs.

Zebras call to each other while grazing.

Lion

The lion is the principal predator of the African savannah. Lionesses hunt together, preying on large animals, such as buffalo, zebra, and wildebeest.

Aardvark

The aardvark is a solitary, nocturnal animal. It uses its powerful claws to break into the nests of ants and termites, which it extracts with its long, sticky tongue. The aardvark can dig at an astonishing speed – faster than a person with a shovel.

Zebra

Zebras usually live in family groups of 5–20 animals, but in the dry season they may gather in herds of a few hundred, for protection against predators such as lions. Male zebras defend themselves by kicking out with their legs and hooves. Zebras eat the tough tops of the grasses.

Papyrus

The most common plant in African swamps is papyrus. It grows in clumps, often dense enough to support the weight of large animals.

Papyrus may reach 4.5 m (15 ft) in height.

Wetland wildlife

Africa's wetlands are seething with wildlife, such as crocodiles, hippos, floodplain species such as lechwes, and fish, including the Nile perch and tiger fish. The wetlands also provide stopping places for migratory birds flying south to winter in Africa.

Lesser flamingo

Three million flamingos gather at Lake Nakuru, in Kenya, forming an amazing spectacle. They feed on the plentiful algae that flourish in the salty water, sunlight, and high temperatures in and around the lake.

Hippopotamus

Hippos spend most of the day submerged in water, with only their ears, eyes, and nostrils above the surface. They become active at dusk when they emerge from the water to graze on nearby grassland.

Long legs for wading through water.

Cichlid fish

Lakes Malawi and Tanganyika contain 265 different species of cichlid (mouth-brooding fish); all but five are unique to Africa. Great depth, isolation, and few predators have resulted in this proliferation.

Webbed feet

A

Addax

The addax lives in the driest and hottest parts of the Sahara – conditions few other animals could tolerate. It rarely drinks as it obtains all its liquid from the succulent plants and tubers on which it feeds.

Pale coat provides camouflage in the desert.

Desert wildlife

The African deserts include the Sahara, the world's largest desert, and the deserts of the Horn of Africa, Kalahari, and Namib. Though the deserts seem barren, they are home to many animals such as bustards, sandgrouse, and the scimitar-horned oryx.

Fennec fox

The fennec lives in small colonies among sand dunes, into which it burrows to avoid the heat. It burrows so quickly, it disappears from sight in seconds.

Fox obtains all its liquid from its prey.

Sand skink

The sand skink spends most of its life underground in its burrow. It uses its flattened tail to propel itself through the sand. It preys on small mammals such as mice, as well as birds' eggs. If attacked, the sand skink can shed its tail, confusing its attacker and enabling it to get away.

Sandgrouse

Despite living in the open desert, sandgrouse must drink regularly. This often means flying long distances. Sandgrouse obtain water for their young by immersing themselves in water and carrying droplets back to their nests in their feathers.

Rainforest wildlife

Rainforests dominate western Central Africa. The warm, wet environment is home to many animals. Herbivores such as gorillas feed on leaves. Fruit that falls from the canopy provides food for pigs and porcupines, while animals such as tree pangolins forage in the trees.

Yellow-backed duiker

Standing 1 m (3.3 ft) at the shoulder, the yellow-backed duiker is the largest of the forest duikers. In West Africa it lives in the densest parts of the rain forest; in East Africa it lives in bamboo forests.

Yellow back patch

Red colobus monkey

The red colobus is one of five species of specialized leaf-eating primates spread across Africa. It lives in the forest canopy in family groups of about 20 animals, rarely descending to the ground.

Small spotted genet

This cat-like animal spends the day asleep in the branches of a tree, becoming active at night. An agile climber, it stalks its prey – birds, small mammals, and insects – like a cat, before seizing it with a sudden pounce.

Gorillas eat many types of rainforest vegetation.

Mountain gorilla

The mountain gorilla is confined to a small area of rainforest, at a point where the boundaries of Uganda, Zaire, and Rwanda meet. It is a massively built animal, but is not normally aggressive. The females build nests where they sleep with their young.

Gelada

The gelada is the sole survivor of a group of ground-dwelling primates now found only in Ethiopia. It lives in open country at high altitude, close to cliffs and rock faces, where it retreats if alarmed. It eats seeds, roots, grass, and fruit.

Mountain wildlife

The mountains of Ruwenzori, Kenya, and Kilimanjaro have distinctive plants and animals. Rodents inhabit moorland, while the scarlet-tufted malachite sunbird lives in close association with giant lobelias.

Giant plants

Africa's mountain plants include some of the most extraordinary vegetation in the world. Plants small elsewhere have grown into giants, including the giant lobelia, tree heath, and giant groundsel, which reaches 9 m (30 ft) in height.

Geladas have a patch of red skin on the chest.

Hyraxes bask in the sun for much of the day.

Flower spikes of the Giant Lobelia are more than 1 m (3.3 ft) tall.

Rock hyrax

Rock hyraxes live in colonies of 50 or more among rocky outcrops. They remain alert for signs of danger, such as eagles and leopards.

Crowned hawk eagle

One of the largest eagles, the crowned hawk eagle is widely distributed throughout the mountainous regions of East Africa and Zaire, wherever there are suitable forests containing the monkeys that are its chief food.

| FIND OUT MORE | BIRDS | BIRDS OF PREY | DEER AND ANTELOPES | GIRAFFES | HIPPOPOTAMUSES | LIONS AND OTHER WILD CATS | LIZARDS | MONKEYS AND OTHER PRIMATES |

AIR

WE LIVE, MOVE, AND BREATHE at the bottom of an immense ocean of air called the atmosphere. Air is an invisible mixture of gases, made up of a teeming mass of millions of tiny gas molecules that move about randomly and at high speed. Without air, the Earth would be a lifeless planet, because the gases air contains are vital to plants and animals.

Fractional distillation
The gases in air have many uses. For example, divers use tanks of oxygen to enable them to breathe underwater, and nitrogen is used in explosives. Gases are extracted from air by a process called fractional distillation. Air is cooled and compressed until it forms a blue liquid. When the liquid expands and warms up, each gas boils off at a different temperature and is collected separately.

Divers with oxygen tanks

Composition of air
Any volume of pure, dry air is 78.09% nitrogen, 20.95% oxygen, 0.93% argon, and 0.03% carbon dioxide and other gases. These coloured balls represent the proportions of the different gases in air.

Candle burns in jar of air.

Flame goes out and water level rises as the oxygen is used up.

Carbon dioxide (CO_2)

Carbon dioxide is vital for plant life. Plants absorb carbon dioxide from the air and combine it with water gathered by their roots to form sugars, which they use for growth.

Tablets of nitrogen fertilizer

Red balls represent oxygen.

Green balls represent argon.

Black ball represents carbon dioxide and other gases.

Blue balls represent nitrogen.

Oxygen (O_2)
Burning is a chemical reaction of a substance with oxygen, as this experiment shows. The candle burns in the jar of air until it has used up all the oxygen. Humans and other animals use oxygen from the air to "burn" food inside their bodies and produce energy.

Nitrogen (N_2)
Every living cell contains nitrogen. Plants cannot take nitrogen from the air, so they get it from the soil. Fertilizers contain nitrogen to replenish what plants remove from the soil.

Argon (Ar)
The gas argon is called an "inert" gas because it is so unreactive. Electric light bulbs are often filled with argon. It prevents the bulb's filament from burning up as it would in air, giving the bulb a much longer life.

Air pollution
Air is not naturally "pure" and contains varying amounts of other substances, such as dust, water vapour, bacteria, pollen, and polluting gases. Air pollution from industry and traffic can cause serious health problems in towns and cities, as well as long-term damage to the environment.

Smog
The hazy air pollution that hangs over an urban area is called smog. Sulphurous smog is the result of burning fuels with a high sulphur content, such as coal. Photochemical smog occurs when sunlight causes car exhaust fumes to react together.

Water vapour
Up to 4 per cent of the volume of air may be water vapour. Warm air can hold more water vapour than cool air. A can of cold drink absorbs heat from the air around it. As the air cools, water vapour condenses out of the air to form droplets on the outside of the can.

Air pressure
Air exerts a force on objects because its moving molecules are constantly colliding with them. Air pressure is a measure of this force. The pressure of the open air is called atmospheric pressure. It is lower at high altitudes, where the air is less dense.

Barometer
A device that measures atmospheric pressure is called a barometer. It can be used to forecast a change in the weather, because air pressure varies slightly from day to day with changes in the air's temperature and humidity.

Sucking

When a person sucks on one end of a drinking straw, the lungs reduce the air pressure inside the straw. Atmospheric pressure on the liquid's surface does the rest, pushing down on the liquid, and making it rise up through the straw.

Compressed air

The pressure of air can be increased by compressing it – that is, pumping more and more of it into a limited space. Bicycle tyres are filled with compressed air to give a smooth, comfortable ride.

Weight of air
Air has weight, as this simple experiment proves. Identical empty balloons are attached to both ends of a stick. The balloons balance when the stick is suspended from its middle. Inflating one of the balloons tips the balance, because the balloon full of compressed air weighs more than the empty balloon.

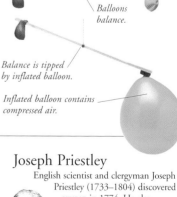

Balloons balance.

Balance is tipped by inflated balloon.

Inflated balloon contains compressed air.

Joseph Priestley

English scientist and clergyman Joseph Priestley (1733–1804) discovered oxygen in 1774. He also discovered many other gases, including nitrous oxide (laughing gas) and ammonia. Priestley studied carbon dioxide and devised a way to make carbonated (fizzy) water.

FIND OUT MORE   ATOMS AND MOLECULES   CELLS   FRICTION   GASES   LUNGS AND BREATHING   PHOTOSYNTHESIS   POLLUTION   PRESSURE   WEATHER

AIRCRAFT

ANY VEHICLE THAT travels through the air is called an aircraft. The ability to soar over obstacles such as oceans and mountains makes aircraft the fastest form of travel. An airliner (a large passenger plane) can fly a passenger thousands of kilometres in hours. The same journey would take several days by boat or car. Airliners and military aircraft are complex machines. Their frames are built with lightweight metals, such as aluminium, and hi-tech materials, such as plastics. Inside, their sophisticated electronic controls help pilots fly efficiently and safely. Smaller aircraft, such as gliders and hot-air balloons, are often used for sport and leisure.

Anatomy of an airliner

Most airliners, such as this *Boeing 747-400*, have the same basic design. The main part is the fuselage, which is similar to a long, thin, metal tube. The wings are attached to the middle of the fuselage, and the tailplane and fin are attached at the back. A floor separates the passenger cabin from the baggage hold.

Types of aircraft

The word aircraft covers all flying machines – from balloons to helicopters. Most aircraft are aeroplanes, which have wings, and jet engines to give them speed. Other types of aircraft are gliders, which have no engines, helicopters, balloons, and airships. An aircraft's function determines its size and shape.

Biplanes
Many planes before World War II (1939–1945) had two pairs of wings, and were called biplanes.

Transport aircraft
Armies need aircraft to transport troops and equipment. Special aircraft are designed to carry very heavy objects, such as tanks.

Balloons
Lighter-than-air craft are known as balloons. A bag is filled with gas or hot air that is lighter than the atmosphere.

Gliders
Currents of air move up and down. A glider has no engine, but flies by the effects of air currents on its wings.

Concorde
Supersonic airliners such as Concorde can travel faster than the speed of sound – about 1,240 kmh (770 mph). They can cross the Atlantic twice as fast as any other airliner, but are very noisy and need lots of fuel.

The Boeing 747-400 can fly more than 13,600 km (8,451 miles) without stopping for fuel.

Fuselage

Upper deck with business-class seats

Main cabin, with economy-class seats

Fin

Tailplane

Fuel for engines in fuel tanks inside wings

Freighters
Airplanes that carry cargo are called freighters. The cargo is loaded through a huge door in the aeroplane's nose. The *Boeing 747* can be converted from a passenger plane to a freighter, then back again.

Forward cabin with first-class seats

Engine controls and navigation instruments

Pilot's control column

Turbofan engines hang from wings on pylons.

Cockpit
The aircraft is controlled from the cockpit. The pilot and co-pilot fly the plane using control columns, and instruments show the status of all the plane's equipment. The cockpit also contains radar and radio controls.

In-flight food
Pre-prepared meals are stored in trolleys, which lock into spaces in the aircraft's galleys until it is time for the cabin staff to serve them.

Entertainment
Some airliners feature video screens and headphones that can be tuned to music channels.

Howard Hughes
Hughes (1905–76) was an American industrialist, film-maker, and aviation enthusiast. He founded the airline TWA, and broke a number of aviation records in aircraft of his own design. Not all were successful; the *Spruce Goose* (1947) only flew once.

Forces of flight

An aircraft needs two forces to fly: lift to keep it up and thrust to propel it forward. Lift overcomes the plane's weight, and thrust overcomes the drag caused by the air flowing past the plane. When an aircraft is cruising, lift is equal to weight and thrust is equal to drag.

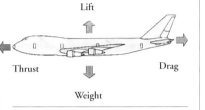

Lift

Thrust

Drag

Weight

Wings

An aircraft's wings create lift. To do this, they need air to flow over them.

The aerofoil shape
If you cut an aircraft wing in two and looked at the end, you would see a special cross-section called an aerofoil. The top surface is longer and more curved than the bottom surface.

The aerofoil at work
The air pressure beneath the wing is greater than above it, and lifts the wing up.

Lift

Angle of attack
Tilting the angle of the blades gives extra lift.

Lift

Flying controls

An aircraft is steered through the air by way of three main control surfaces – the elevators on the tailplane, the ailerons on the wings, and a rudder on the fin.

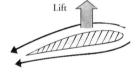

Elevators make the aircraft's nose tilt up and down.

Ailerons make the aircraft roll from side to side.

The rudder makes the aircraft "yaw" to left or right.

Aero engines

An aircraft's engines drive it through the air by producing thrust. Different types of engine produce thrust in different ways. Piston and turbo-prop engines drive propellers that screw into the air, just as a ship propeller bites into water. Turbo-jet and turbo-fan engines produce a fast-moving stream of gas which pushes the aircraft forwards.

Piston engines
These work in the same way as car engines. Petrol and air vapour are mixed in the engine's cylinders and they cause an explosion. The explosions push pistons, which turn a shaft. The shaft then turns a propeller.

Shaft

Turbo-prop engines
The simplest type of jets – a turbo-jet engine with a propeller is called a turbo-prop engine. A motor turns the compressor and the propeller, which provides the main engine thrust.

Propeller spins to provide engine thrust

Turbo-jet engines
Air is drawn in and compressed, then sent to a chamber where fuel burns. The gases produced are shot out of the back of the engine, which pushes the aircraft forwards, like a deflating balloon.

Gas shoots out

Air drawn in

Turbo-fan engines
A hybrid of turbo-jet and turbo-props, the turbo-fan engine sucks in air, which is combined with the backdraft from a fan, and also sends air around the engine, producing the same effect as a propeller.

Turbo fan

Exhaust

Helicopters

Unlike most aircraft, which have fixed wings, a helicopter has a spinning rotor with two or more long, thin blades attached. When the blades spin round, they lift the helicopter straight up into the air. A helicopter can take off from almost anywhere and does not need to use airport runways. It can hover in one place, and fly backwards, forwards, and sideways. This makes it the most versatile of all aircraft; it is very useful for transport, surveillance, and rescue missions.

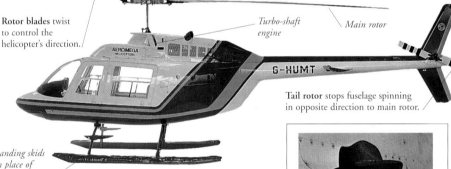

Rotor blades twist to control the helicopter's direction.

Turbo-shaft engine

Main rotor

G-HUMT

Tail rotor stops fuselage spinning in opposite direction to main rotor.

Landing skids in place of undercarriage

Flying controls
A helicopter pilot has three flying controls. The collective pitch lever changes the amount of lift produced by the main rotor. The cyclic pitch control makes the helicopter move forwards, backwards, or sideways. Rudder pedals make the helicopter turn left or right.

Lifting off
Before take-off, the main and tail rotors are speeded up. When the main rotor is turning fast enough, the pilot lifts the collective pitch lever to increase the tilt of the rotor blades. The tilt produces lift, and the aircraft takes off. The higher the lever is lifted, the faster the aircraft rises.

Moving away
The cyclic pitch control makes the helicopter move in the direction the control is pushed. It tilts the main rotor so that some of the rotor's lift pulls the helicopter along. Here, the pilot has pulled the control back to make the helicopter move backwards.

Igor Ivan Sikorsky
Sikorsky (1889–1972) was born in Ukraine, where he became an aeronautical engineer. In 1919 he moved to the United States where he set up an aircraft factory. He designed the first practical helicopter, the VS-300, which first flew in 1939. The design had to be modified many times: at one point, the helicopter flew in every direction except forwards.

FIND OUT MORE   AIRSHIPS AND BALLOONS   ATMOSPHERE   ENGINES AND MOTORS   FLIGHT, HISTORY OF   TRANSPORT, HISTORY OF   WARPLANES   WORLD WAR I   WORLD WAR II

Types of aircraft

Military

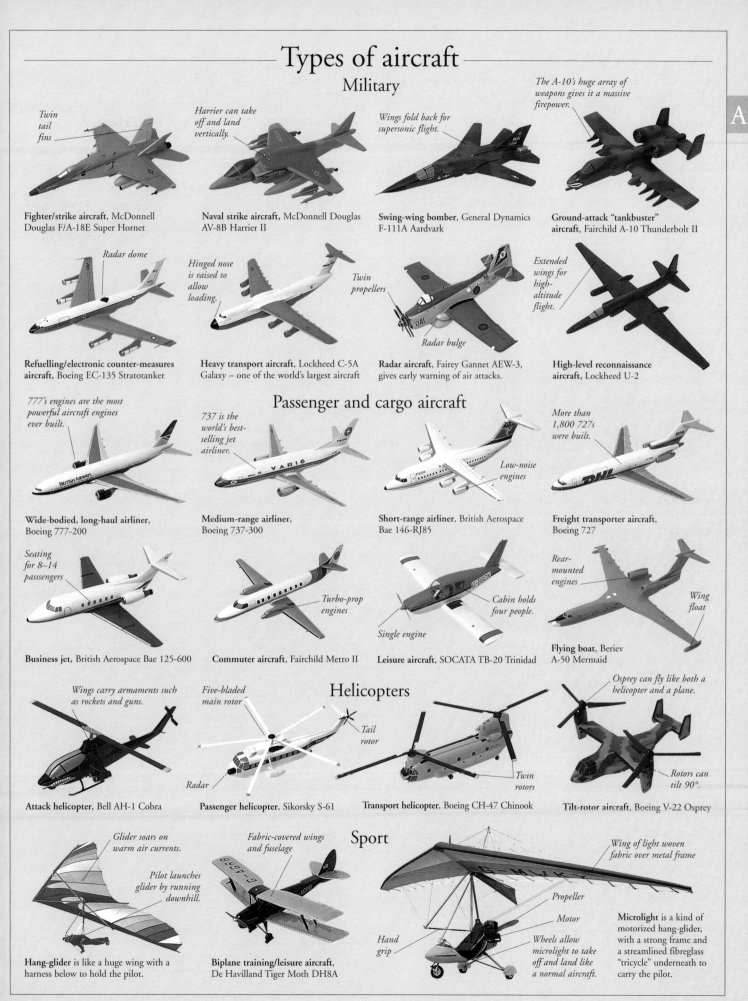

Fighter/strike aircraft, McDonnell Douglas F/A-18E Super Hornet

Twin tail fins

Naval strike aircraft, McDonnell Douglas AV-8B Harrier II

Harrier can take off and land vertically.

Swing-wing bomber, General Dynamics F-111A Aardvark

Wings fold back for supersonic flight.

Ground-attack "tankbuster" aircraft, Fairchild A-10 Thunderbolt II

The A-10's huge array of weapons gives it a massive firepower.

Refuelling/electronic counter-measures aircraft, Boeing EC-135 Stratotanker

Radar dome

Heavy transport aircraft, Lockheed C-5A Galaxy – one of the world's largest aircraft

Hinged nose is raised to allow loading.

Radar aircraft, Fairey Gannet AEW-3, gives early warning of air attacks.

Twin propellers

Radar bulge

High-level reconnaissance aircraft, Lockheed U-2

Extended wings for high-altitude flight.

Passenger and cargo aircraft

Wide-bodied, long-haul airliner, Boeing 777-200

777's engines are the most powerful aircraft engines ever built.

Medium-range airliner, Boeing 737-300

737 is the world's best-selling jet airliner.

Short-range airliner, British Aerospace Bae 146-RJ85

Low-noise engines

Freight transporter aircraft, Boeing 727

More than 1,800 727s were built.

Business jet, British Aerospace Bae 125-600

Seating for 8–14 passsengers

Commuter aircraft, Fairchild Metro II

Turbo-prop engines

Leisure aircraft, SOCATA TB-20 Trinidad

Single engine

Cabin holds four people.

Flying boat, Beriev A-50 Mermaid

Rear-mounted engines

Wing float

Helicopters

Attack helicopter, Bell AH-1 Cobra

Wings carry armaments such as rockets and guns.

Passenger helicopter, Sikorsky S-61

Five-bladed main rotor

Tail rotor

Radar

Transport helicopter, Boeing CH-47 Chinook

Twin rotors

Tilt-rotor aircraft, Boeing V-22 Osprey

Osprey can fly like both a helicopter and a plane.

Rotors can tilt 90°.

Sport

Hang-glider is like a huge wing with a harness below to hold the pilot.

Glider soars on warm air currents.

Pilot launches glider by running downhill.

Biplane training/leisure aircraft, De Havilland Tiger Moth DH8A

Fabric-covered wings and fuselage

Wing of light woven fabric over metal frame

Hand grip

Propeller

Motor

Wheels allow microlight to take off and land like a normal aircraft.

Microlight is a kind of motorized hang-glider, with a strong frame and a streamlined fibreglass "tricycle" underneath to carry the pilot.

AIRPORTS

TODAY, MORE PEOPLE TRAVEL by air than ever before. Whether they are business people off to visit clients or families going on holiday, all air travellers leave from airports, which range in size from small local facilities to enormous international terminals. A large airport is like a city. It contains shops, offices, and hotels, in addition to all the buildings, runways, and taxiways needed to service the aircraft and their passengers. Airport security is always tight, because airports and aircraft have often been the targets of terrorist attacks.

Features of an airport

Aircraft take off and land on runways, which are linked to the terminal buildings by routes called taxiways. The passengers embark and disembark at the terminal buildings. For the aircraft, the airport has repair workshops, refuelling facilities, and storage hangars.

Runway
To take the biggest jet aircraft, runways have to be 3–4 km (1.8–2.5 miles) long and some 50 m (165 ft) wide. They need a specially toughened surface to take the pounding they get when large jets take off or land.

Terminal building at Kansai International Airport, Japan

"Landside" of terminal

Passengers enter terminal from lower level and leave it from upper level.

Road transport for passengers leaving the airport.

Access area provides escalators to all parts of the terminal building.

International arrivals floor

Curving roof truss

International departures floor

Security area and passport checkpoint

Domestic arrivals and departures are on middle 2 floors.

Boarding gates

"Airside" of terminal

Bridge connects boarding gate to aircraft.

Waiting aircraft

Service area contains boilers, ventilation equipment, and other building services.

Air traffic control

At the heart of an airport is the control tower, where air traffic controllers monitor every moment of an aircraft's arrival and departure. They make sure that each pilot follows the correct flight path, that all aircraft land in the right place, and that there is a safe amount of time between each take-off and landing.

Air traffic controllers in the control tower

Radar display screen
Airport radar tracks each aircraft as it lands, giving the controllers precise details of its position. All aircraft within 20 to 50 km (12 to 30 miles) of the airport can be tracked by radar and shown on the controllers' display screens.

Flight path
Air traffic controllers tell pilots when it is safe to land. They guide a pilot to a specific path, which the pilot must then follow as the aircraft descends to the runway. Navigation aids, such as high-frequency radio beacons, give the pilot accurate bearings.

How an aircraft lands

Fly down and right

Course is correct

Runway (ground level)

Fly up and left

Radar antenna sends out beam to guide plane on to runway.

Flight path

Antenna sends out beam to guide plane's rate of descent.

Radio waves carry information about flight path.

Dials on flight-deck tell pilot whether plane's course is correct.

Security

Airport security staff are always on their guard, trying to spot terrorists or smugglers. Metal detectors and other electronic devices alert staff when a passenger is carrying a gun or other type of weapon. There are also "sniffer" dogs that have been trained to detect the scent of explosives or illegal drugs.

Passports
A person travelling from one country to another usually carries a passport, an official document that identifies the owner and their place of origin. Passports are inspected at international airports.

EU passport

An X-ray reveals a gun.

X-ray scanner
Airport staff use X-ray machines to scan the contents of passengers' luggage. A screen on the side of the X-ray machine shows what is inside each bag. Different materials show up in different colours, enabling items such as guns to be found with ease.

Airports and the environment

A large airport can have a devastating impact on the local environment. Clearing the land to build an airport destroys carefully balanced ecosystems, while the air pollution can harm wildlife, and the noise may scare some animals away.

Kestrel

Airport ecosystems
Since airports cover such vast areas, birds and animals can also move into these areas and establish new ecosystems, undisturbed by people.

Animals can live in the large green spaces around a big airport.

FIND OUT MORE

AIRCRAFT

ECOLOGY AND ECOSYSTEMS

RADAR AND SONAR

TRAVEL

AIRSHIPS AND BALLOONS

AIRSHIPS AND BALLOONS are known as lighter-than-air aircraft because, instead of wings, they use a large envelope, or bag, full of gas or hot air that is lighter than the air in the atmosphere around it. The air pushes the envelope upwards, just as water pushes a submerged air-filled ball upwards. In 1783, the Montgolfier brothers achieved the first manned flight ever by sending a hot-air balloon over Paris. Balloons fly where the wind blows them; airships have engines and can be steered. Today, airships are used for aerial filming and coast-guard patrols, and ballooning is a popular sport.

Anatomy of a modern airship

The main part of an airship is its envelope, which contains bags of helium gas. The gas is slightly pressurized to keep the envelope in shape. A fin and tailplane keep the airship steady as it flies slowly along. The crew travels in a gondola attached to the underside of the envelope.

Gas-proof coated polyester envelope *Elevator flaps*

Automatic ballonet valve *Gondola* Skyship 500 HL (semirigid airship) *Rudder to steer the airship.*

Airship disasters
The Hindenburg, 1937

Several terrible disasters made people lose trust in airship travel. Airships were usually lost for two reasons: either they were uncontrollable in bad weather; or the highly inflammable hydrogen gas used inside the envelope exploded. Today, airship pilots use the much safer helium gas in special nylon envelopes. However, they still have to be wary of the weather.

Types of airship

Practical airships could be built only after the lightweight internal combustion engine had been developed. The earliest airships were "nonrigid" (they are still used today). These were followed by the "rigid" and the less usual "semirigid" types of airship.

Nonrigid airships have a flexible fabric envelope, from which the load hangs, suspended by ropes.

Rigid airship's envelope is built around a rigid framework. This skeleton contains bags of the lifting gas – helium.

Ferdinand von Zeppelin

German count Ferdinand von Zeppelin (1838–1917) began experimenting with air travel in 1891. In 1900, he devised the first airship, a 128-m (420-ft) rigid craft named the LZ1. During World War I, some 100 Zeppelins were built for military use.

Balloons

Balloons were first used for aerial reconnaissance during the French Revolution, and used again in the American Civil War. During World Wars I and II, balloons were used to spot targets for artillery attacks, and barrage balloons defended cities against aircraft.

Weather and research balloons
To study what is happening in the upper reaches of the atmosphere, pilots send up helium-filled weather balloons. These carry instruments which measure temperature, wind speed, and so on, and send their results to the ground or to satellites by radio.

Balloon festivals
Today, ballooning is a popular sport. During the summer, ballooning enthusiasts gather at festivals to enjoy the dazzling prospect of dozens of brightly coloured balloons flying together. Some of the balloons are owned by companies, and are made in the shapes of their products, as a form of advertising.

Flight

Hot-air ballooning requires a perfectly clear day with a gentle breeze. Too high a wind puts the balloon at risk on take-off and landing. After take-off, a ground crew follows the balloon in a vehicle to recover both it and the crew after landing.

1 The balloon is laid on the ground. Burners heat air to fill the balloon.

2 The balloon's envelope expands as the hot air starts to fill it.

3 The expanding balloon becomes buoyant, and rises into the air.

4 Guy ropes hold the balloon down until the crew boards.

5 The crew blasts hot air into the envelope to keep the balloon afloat.

| FIND OUT MORE | ATMOSPHERE | FLIGHT, HISTORY OF | GALILEO GALILEI | GASES | JOHNSON, AMY | RENAISSANCE | WEATHER FORECASTING |

Airships and balloons

Balloons

False basket

Lavishly decorated character from the *Thousand and One Nights*

Easter egg envelope is decorated to celebrate Easter.

Golf ball, an uncomplicated, yet realistic balloon shape

Upside-down balloon, where a false basket has been attached to the balloon's top.

Fabergé egg, the trademark jewel of a famous Russian jewellers

Basket

Part of this balloon hangs below the basket.

Red, blue, and yellow panels of this balloon's envelope represent the exotic plumage of a parrot.

Carmen Miranda, a 1940s' singing star

Uncle Sam, a lighthearted symbol of the USA

Moon

A **"cow jumps over the moon"** is a very complicated balloon shape inspired by the famous nursery rhyme.

Face-shaped balloons are relatively simple to create.

Upturned eaves

Modern tractor has its basket hanging where the back axle would be.

Drink can, the first non-traditional balloon shape

Santa Claus, an aerial Christmas decoration

NASA rocket, celebrating space exploration.

Elephant, complete with trunk and a surprised look!

Japanese temple; the envelope comes complete with authentic upturned eaves and balcony rails.

Airships

Spectacular eagle has a very complicated and realistically painted envelope.

Aerial tours are often run by companies that have both airships and balloons.

Modern airships, because of their visibility and size, are often used to advertise products or services.

Rupert the Bear, a favourite fictional character for children all over the world

ALEXANDER THE GREAT

IN LESS THAN FOUR YEARS, a brilliant young general created the largest empire the world had ever seen. The empire was the creation of Alexander the Great of Macedon, a gifted leader who inspired tremendous loyalty from his troops. It stretched from Greece in the west to India in the east. Alexander's sudden death at the age of 33 led to the empire's collapse, but it lived on in a series of towns that spread Greek culture eastwards. These cities, all called Alexandria after their founder, opened up a trade between Asia and Europe that survived for centuries.

Early life
Alexander was born in 356 BC, the son of King Philip II of Macedon (r. 359–336 BC). As a young man he went on military campaigns with his father. Alexander won fame for taming a wild black horse called Bucephalus, which stayed with him throughout his whole life.

Aristotle
Alexander was taught by the Athenian philosopher Aristotle (384–322 BC). Aristotle's interests ranged from politics and morality to biology and literature. He shared his enthusiasm for new ideas with his young pupil.

A

Alexander's empire
When Alexander became king of Macedon in 336 BC, Greece was dominated by Persia. In a series of brilliant military campaigns, Alexander defeated Persia and created his vast empire.

Greece
The heartland of Alexander's empire was his home state of Macedon, northern Greece. Before Alexander became king, Greece was divided into rival city states, and was threatened by the powerful Persian Empire.

Terracotta figure of the Greek love goddess, Aphrodite

Persia
The rich empire of Persia occupied much of modern Iraq, Turkey, and Iran. After Alexander had conquered the area, he tried to unite Macedonia and Persia by encouraging his generals to marry Persians. Alexander himself married Roxana, a princess from eastern Persia.

Stag comes from palace at Persepolis.

• Gordion
• Issus
• Gaugamela
Alexandria ad Caucasum
Alexandria Prophthasia
• Alexandria   Babylon
• Persepolis

☐ Macedonian Empire

Persian silver stag ornament

Egypt
In 332 BC, Alexander conquered Egypt and was accepted as the new pharaoh. He founded the city of Alexandria, in northern Egypt, which became the most important city of the Greek-speaking world. When Alexander died in 323 BC, he was buried in a vast tomb in the centre of the city.

Alexander wears the pharaoh's crown

Battle of Issus
In 333 BC, the Macedonian army overwhelmed the more powerful Persian army led by Darius III (r. 336–330 BC) at the battle of Issus, Syria. The Persians were defeated again in 331 BC at Gaugamela near the River Tigris. After this battle, the Persian capital, Persepolis, was destroyed and the empire collapsed.

Relief of the Battle of Issus

Eastern empire
By 326 BC, Alexander had marched through Persia and had conquered Afghanistan and the Punjab. Although his troops were very loyal to him, they refused to go further than the River Indus.

Coin from Indus area

Death of Alexander
In 323 BC Alexander caught a fever in the city of Babylon. Although he was only 33, he died. This sudden death meant that Alexander did not have time to consolidate his rule or even name his successor. Within a few years of his death, the huge Macedonian Empire had collapsed.

Alexander's sarcophagus

Carved relief shows Alexander leading his troops.

Sarcophagus from the royal cemetery of Sidon, said to be the tomb of Alexander.

ALEXANDER THE GREAT

356 BC	Born in Macedon
336 BC	Succeeds his father to the Macedonian throne; quells rebellions in Greece
334 BC	Leads his army into Persia and defeats a Persian army at the Granicus River
333 BC	Defeats Darius III at Issus
331 BC	Defeats Darius III again at Gaugamela, completing his conquest of the Persian Empire
326 BC	Reaches the Indus, but is forced to turn back by his troops
323 BC	Dies of fever in Babylon

FIND OUT MORE

ASIA, HISTORY OF · EGYPT, ANCIENT · GREECE, ANCIENT · PERSIAN EMPIRES · PHILOSOPHY

A

AMERICAN CIVIL WAR

LESS THAN 80 YEARS after independence, the USA split in two over the issue of slavery. The richer, industrial northern states had banned slavery, but slaves were used on plantations in the south. When Abraham Lincoln became president in 1860, the southern states, fearing he would ban slavery, seceded from the Union, and established the Confederate States of America. Fighting began in 1861 and lasted for four years. At first the sides were evenly matched, but the strength of the Union wore down the Confederacy, and it surrendered. Slavery was then abolished throughout the country.

Divided nation

Eleven southern slave states left the Union of states, declaring independence as the Confederacy. Four other slave states refused to break away; West Virginia split from the rest of the state and stayed in the Union.

Slave states in the union

Confederate states

Union states

Washington

Charleston

First modern war

The American Civil War was the first recognizably modern war. Railways transported men and supplies to the battlefield, and iron ships were used for the first time. Commanders talked to each other by field telegraph, and the war was photographed and widely reported in newspapers.

Much of the fighting was trench warfare, but troops were also prepared for a pitched battle.

Union soldiers and guns

Gunner

Field gun

Officer

Soldiers
More than three million people fought in the two opposing armies, most of them as infantrymen (foot soldiers).

Union infantry sergeant

Chevrons

Shell jacket

Sergeant's sash

Sergeant's trouser stripe

Percussion musket

Confederate infantryman

Abraham Lincoln
Lincoln was born in Kentucky in 1809. He was elected to the state legislature in 1834, was elected president in 1860, and led the Union states to victory in the civil war. He was assassinated in 1865.

Merrimack and Monitor
The Confederate ironclad ship *Merrimack* (renamed *Virginia*) fought the Union's vessel *Monitor* on 9 March 1862. The battle was inconclusive, but marked the first occasion on which iron ships had been used in naval warfare.

Gettysburg Address
Lincoln's fine speeches helped win the war. In 1863, he dedicated a cemetery on the site of a battlefield in Gettysburg, Pennsylvania. In his speech, he hoped that "these dead shall not have died in vain; that this nation, under God, shall have a new birth of freedom, and that government of the people, by the people, for the people, shall not perish from the earth".

Appomattox
On 9 April 1865, at Appomattox, Virginia, the Confederate general Robert E. Lee surrendered to Union general Ulysses S. Grant. More than 600,000 Americans died in the four years of fighting, and many more were injured.

Signing the surrender documents

Timeline

April 1861 After 11 states leave the Union, war breaks out when Confederate troops fire on the Union garrison at Fort Sumter, South Carolina.

1861 Confederates under generals Jackson and Beauregard win the first major battle against Unionists at Bull Run, near Washington.

1862 Confederates win Seven Days' Battle (near Richmond, Virginia) and Battle of Fredericksburg, Virginia.

1863 Union wins its first major battle at Gettysburg; Emancipation Proclamation frees slaves.

Ulysses S. Grant

1864 Ulysses S. Grant becomes Union commander-in-chief.

1864 General Sherman's Union army marches through Georgia, destroying the state capital and weakening the Confederacy.

Civil War cannon

April 1865 Lee's Confederate army surrenders at Appomattox, Virginia.

May 1865 Last Confederate army surrenders.

December 1865 Slavery is banned throughout the USA by the 13th amendment.

FIND OUT MORE   AMERICAN REVOLUTION   ARMIES   NORTH AMERICA, HISTORY OF   SHIPS AND BOATS   SLAVERY   UNITED STATES, HISTORY OF   WARFARE   WASHINGTON, GEORGE

AMERICAN REVOLUTION

IN 1783, A NEW NATION WAS BORN – the United States of America. Its struggle for independence is called the American Revolution. It began in 1775, when 13 American colonies went to war against Britain. Britain governed the colonies and imposed high taxes. The colonists, who were not represented in the British Parliament, resented the taxes. Protests and demonstrations broke out, and the colonists formed a Continental Congress to negotiate with Britain. A skirmish led to war, and in 1776, the American colonists, inspired by ideals of freedom, declared independence. The British surrendered in 1781, and two years later recognized the new country.

Maine (to Massachusetts)
New Hampshire
Massachusetts
New York
Pennsylvania
Rhode Island
Connecticut
New Jersey
Delaware
Virginia
Maryland
N. Carolina
S. Carolina
Georgia

Thirteen colonies
After the Revolution, Britain's 13 original colonies formed the first 13 states of the new United States.

Stamp tax

The colonists set their own taxes. But in 1765, Britain introduced a stamp tax on legal documents. The angry colonists stated that "taxation without representation is tyranny". They refused to buy British goods.

Boston Tea Party
Britain withdrew the stamp tax, but set others on glass and tea. Three groups of protesters, dressed as Mohawk Indians, boarded tea ships in Boston Harbour and threw their cargo into the water.

Colonists pour tea into Boston Harbour, in protest at British taxes

Lexington and Concord

In April 1775, the war began with skirmishes near Lexington and Concord. American patriots forced the British to withdraw at Lexington. They marched back to Boston under continuous fire.

Paul Revere
Paul Revere (1735–1818) rode through Massachusetts on the night of 18 April 1775, to warn that the British were coming. He was part of an anti-British group called the Sons of Liberty.

Revere on horseback

Thomas Jefferson

A planter from Virginia, Thomas Jefferson (1743–1826) attended the Continental Congress in 1775. He drafted the Declaration of Independence, reformed the laws of his native state, and went on diplomatic missions to Europe. He became the third president of the USA in 1801 and served until 1809.

Surrender at Yorktown
The fighting lasted until spring 1781, when the colonists cut the British off from their supplies at Yorktown. They finally surrendered on 19 October.

Declaration of Independence
On 4 July 1776, the 13 colonies signed the Declaration of Independence. This document stated that "all men are created equal..." and its belief in "Life, Liberty, and the Pursuit of Happiness" later inspired the French Revolution.

George Washington

The commander of the colonial army was George Washington (1732–1799). He was an inspiring general, who kept the morale of his troops high in spite of several defeats at the beginning of the war. When France joined the war on the colonial side in 1778, followed by Spain in 1779, victory was assured.

Washington

- Cocked hat
- Cartridge box belt
- Knapsack strap
- Brush for musket lock
- Musket
- Gaitered trousers
- Musket

American soldier

- Cocked hat
- Crossbelt
- Red coat
- Bayonet
- Brush for musket lock
- Breeches
- Leather spatterdash
- Shoe

British infantryman

Revolutionary war

The war lasted for six years. Washington's leadership played a vital part in the American victory. He led his troops to victories at Brandywine (1777) and Yorktown (1781).

The opposing armies
The British were well trained but poorly led. Their orders came from 4,000 km (2,500 miles) away. The Americans were less well trained and equipped, but knew the terrain and had good leaders.

Timeline
1765 Britain introduces the stamp tax. Protests break out. Britain withdraws the stamp tax, but other taxes remain.

1773 Boston Tea Party. Americans, dressed as Mohawks, dump tea in Boston Harbour as a protest against heavy taxes.

1774–75 Continental Congress. Representatives draft a petition to Britain insisting on no taxation without representation.

1775 Battle of Lexington. Congress takes over government of the colonies, and appoints Washington Commander-in-Chief.

1777 British general John Burgoyne (1722–92) forced to surrender at Saratoga.

1778 France joins the war on the American side.

1781 British surrender at Yorktown.

French private soldier

FIND OUT MORE FRENCH REVOLUTION UNITED KINGDOM, HISTORY OF UNITED STATES, HISTORY OF WARFARE WASHINGTON, GEORGE

AMPHIBIANS

COLD-BLOODED animals, amphibians are vertebrates (animals with a backbone) that evolved from fish. They are adapted for life on land, but most must return to water in some form to breed. Amphibians undergo a process known as metamorphosis in their development from larvae to adult, hence the Greek origin of their name: *amphi* meaning "double"; *bios* meaning "life". There are three groups of amphibians and more than 3,000 species.

Amphibian features

Apart from the caecilians and a few species of salamander, adult amphibians have four legs, each with four or five digits. Most species take to the water to mate and produce their eggs, but some make nests on land, occasionally in burrows in the ground or in moss.

European common frog

Long legs for leaping.

Frog leaps after prey such as an insect.

Webbed toes for swimming.

Marbled newt

"Marbled" colour extends along the tail.

Amphibian groups

There are three groups of amphibians: the worm-like caecilians; the tailed amphibians, including newts and salamanders; and the tail-less frogs and toads, probably the most diverse group.

Couch's spadefoot toad

Distribution of amphibians
Amphibians live everywhere. Desert species survive the driest season by staying underground inside a membranous sac, which they secrete themselves. Some temperate species hibernate in pond mud in the winter.

Caecilians
Caecilians are legless, carnivorous amphibians most of which live in the tropics. Some species burrow in the ground; others are aquatic. They have small eyes and ears and sensory tentacles on the head.

Frogs and toads
In temperate regions, frogs are more aquatic than toads, have slimier skin and longer legs. In the tropics, some species of frog and toad are fully aquatic and live in trees or underground.

Newts and salamanders
The tailed amphibians – newts, salamanders, and the eel-like sirens of North America – live in tropical forests, temperate woods, mountain streams, and lakes. Some have very specialized lifestyles: a few even live in the total darkness of caves.

Skin

Amphibian skin is thin and scaleless. It is usually kept moist with mucus to increase its ability to allow oxygen through for skin breathing. Skin can be smooth or rough. It secretes certain chemicals: pheromones can attract potential mates, while poisons deter predators. As they grow, amphibians shed the top layer of skin.

White's tree frogs

Colour
Amphibians may have skin colours that absorb or reflect heat. Colour also varies with temperature, becoming pale when warm and darker if cold and damp.

Camouflaged tree frogs

Camouflage
Many frogs and toads are camouflaged to avoid detection by predators. Most have a combination of forest colours and disruptive patterning. Some rainforest species are shaped to look like dead leaves.

Great crested newt   Square marked toad

Mandarin salamander   Tree frog

Texture
Many frogs and toads have smooth skin covered with mucus. Other amphibians, such as the mandarin salamander and many dry-skinned toads, have raised nodules.

Poison-dart tadpoles

Defence
The bright colours of Colombian poison-dart frogs warn predators of their highly toxic skin. The tadpoles develop their skin poisons as their colours develop. Marine toads secrete a strong toxin through large glands behind the head.

Metamorphosis

The development from an aquatic larva that breathes through gills, or spiracles, to an air-breathing adult is called metamorphosis. It involves the growth of legs and the loss of the tail in frogs and toads.

Newt egg

Frog spawn

Eggs
Amphibian eggs are laid singly, in clumps, or in strings of clear "jelly" called spawn. They have no shell and require a moist environment to survive.

Tadpoles
Larvae, or tadpoles, hatch from the eggs. Salamander tadpoles have limbs, but frogs and toads develop these during metamorphosis. Salamander larvae are carnivorous, but most frog and toad tadpoles are herbivorous.

Frog tadpole

Gills

Salamander tadpole

Axolotl
Some salamanders may stay as larvae all their life. The axolotl is a form of the Mexican tiger salamander.

| FIND OUT MORE | EVOLUTION | FROGS AND TOADS | POISONOUS ANIMALS | SALAMANDERS AND NEWTS |

ANGLO-SAXONS

BY THE END of the 8th century, Britain's people, known as the Anglo-Saxons, had created a rich culture, which included masterpieces of jewellery, architecture, and literature. Originally these people had come from northern Germany and southern Denmark, where they were known as the Angles, Saxons, and Jutes. In the 3rd and 4th centuries, these tribes travelled to various parts of the Roman Empire, including Gaul, or present-day France, where their influence was short-lived. They travelled to Britain in the 5th century, where they settled, and formed several separate kingdoms. Eventually the kingdom of Wessex became the dominant power.

Kingdoms

There was always a struggle for supremacy among the kingdoms formed by the settlers. Northumbria was the earliest one to dominate under Edwin (d. 633). Then it was Mercia's turn under Aethelbald (d. 757) and Offa (d. 796). Finally, Wessex dominated under Alfred the Great. When Vikings from Denmark attacked and occupied northern England, Alfred stopped them from pushing farther south, and the Anglo-Saxons reconquered the north in the 10th century.

King Canute the Great

By 1016, the Danes ruled all England under the popular Canute (c.995–1035). Canute's sons inherited England, but the Anglo-Saxon Edward the Confessor (c.1003–1066) regained the country in 1042. He had no children and, when he died, an unsettled England was vulnerable to conquest by the Normans.

Edward the Confessor   Canute the Great

Culture

Cultural life centred on the monasteries and on the royal court. Alfred the Great gathered scholars and artists around him, and he himself translated many of the Latin classics into Anglo-Saxon, or Old English.

Architecture

Anglo-Saxon churches, like the one at Earls Barton, England, often have square towers decorated with stone relief. This pattern may be based on timber buildings of the period, which have all perished.

Decorated manuscripts

Monks produced quality manuscripts. One monk wrote the work, while a second illustrated it with figures, such as St Dunstan (c.909–988) kneeling before Jesus, and a third decorated it.

Possible image of Alfred the Great

Jewellery

This jewel is inscribed "Alfred ordered me to be made" and may have belonged to Alfred the Great. The inscription and animal-head decoration are finely worked in gold; the portrait, perhaps of the king himself, is made of enamel.

Written records

In the 7th century, missionaries from mainland Europe, such as St Augustine of Canterbury, converted the Anglo-Saxons to Christianity. The creation of monasteries meant that more people learned to read and write. Monks produced historical works, such as the *Anglo-Saxon Chronicle*, which today give insights into the events of the period.

Anglo-Saxon Chronicle

In the ninth century, Alfred the Great ordered the *Chronicle*, a year-by-year account of the history of England. It covers the lives of kings and church leaders, military history, and major events, such as the Viking invasions, and was last updated in 1154.

Bede (c.673–735)

Bede, an English monk and teacher in Jarrow, wrote *A History of the English Church and People*, one of the most important sources of our knowledge of Anglo-Saxon times.

Alfred the Great

Ruler of Wessex and Mercia, Alfred (c.849–c.899) was an able soldier who defended his kingdom against the Vikings. He loved learning and education, and arts and crafts flourished in his reign. He could not drive the Vikings from northern England, but most people saw him as their protector. He was the first English king to become a national symbol.

Timeline

450 Angles, Saxons, and Jutes from northern Germany and Denmark begin to arrive in England. They settle mainly along the eastern coast – East Anglia.

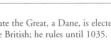

802–39 Reign of Egbert of Wessex. There are many Viking attacks.

871–99 Reign of Alfred the Great, famous for law-making, translating books into Old English, and defeating the Vikings at Edington in 878.

Anglo-Saxon buckle

1016 Canute the Great, a Dane, is elected king by the British; he rules until 1035.

1042 Anglo-Saxons regain power under Edward the Confessor.

1066 Last Anglo-Saxon king, Harold II, is killed by William of Normandy at the Battle of Hastings.

FIND OUT MORE CELTS EUROPE, HISTORY OF MONASTERIES NORMANS UNITED KINGDOM, HISTORY OF VIKINGS

ANIMAL BEHAVIOUR

ALL ANIMALS RESPOND to their surroundings. A cat, for example, will arch its back when threatening a rival, but lower its body when stalking a mouse. Everything that an animal does, and the way in which it does it, makes up its behaviour. An animal's behaviour enables it to increase its chances of survival and find a mate so that it can pass on its genes to the next generation. Some behaviours are inbuilt, or instinctive; others are learned during the animal's lifetime.

Egg-rolling
Greylag geese nest on the ground. If an egg rolls out of the nest, the female goose automatically reaches out with her neck and pulls the egg back in. By being in the wrong place, the egg acts as a sign stimulus that causes the female to carry out the fixed-action pattern of egg-rolling.

Instinctive behaviour

Instinct is a term used to describe behaviours that an animal performs automatically without having to learn them. Instinctive behaviour is programmed by an animal's genes. It consists of unchanging components called fixed-action patterns. The fixed-action pattern often begins when an animal responds to a feature in its surroundings or on another animal, called a sign stimulus.

Web spinning
Many species of spider, including this black widow spider, spin webs in order to trap their insect food. Web spinning is purely instinctive. A spider would not have time in its limited life to learn how to construct such a complex structure.

Sign stimulus
In the spring, when these freshwater fish breed, the male's throat and belly turn red. If one male intrudes into the territory of another male, its red colour acts as a sign stimulus that produces a fixed-action pattern: the occupying fish drives out the intruder.

Bright spring colours

Bright colours fade after the breeding season.

Learned behaviour

Learning occurs when an animal adapts to its surroundings by changing its behaviour. By responding to experiences and adapting to changing conditions, an animal increases its chances of survival. Learning takes time, and animals that are dependent on learned behaviour have long lives and large brains.

Learning tool use
Some animals learn to use simple "tools" in order to feed. Sea otters, found off the coast of California, USA, swim on their backs with a stone on their chests on which they smash the shells of clams and mussels to get at the juicy contents. Young otters learn tool use from their parents.

Trial and error learning
An animal will associate an action it carries out with a successful result, such as getting food or defeating a rival. This "reward" motivates the animal to alter its behaviour to improve the result of future actions.

Puppies play-fight and perfect their hunting skills.

Young ducklings follow their mother.

Imprinting
This is shown by some young animals that make a strong bond with their parent soon after hatching or birth. Young ducklings, for example, stay close to their mother and improve their chances of survival under her protection.

Insight learning
This involves a form of reasoning. Some animals can solve new problems by drawing on past experiences. Chimpanzees, having learned to extract termites or ants from a nest with a stick, can exploit any shape or size of nest.

Communication

Animals communicate by sending out signals that are recognized by other animals and alter their behaviour in some way. The signals can be sights, sounds, or scents. Communication is used, for example, to find a mate, threaten rivals or enemies, defend a territory, warn of danger, or hold a group together.

Song thrush sings from a perch.

Visual signals
Animals may use visual signals as a threat or to attract a mate. This puss moth caterpillar adopts a warning posture if threatened by an enemy. An enemy that ignores the warning is rewarded with a stinging squirt of formic acid.

Puss moth caterpillar

Bright colours add to the warning.

Sound
Many animals, including crickets, bullfrogs, peacocks, and whales, use sound to communicate. This male song thrush sings to proclaim his territory, to warn rivals to stay away, and to attract a female.

Chemicals
Some animals release chemicals called pheromones, which, when detected, affect the behaviour of other members of the same species. Female gypsy moths release pheromones that attract males from several kilometres away.

Gypsy moth

Courtship

Mating in most mammals and birds takes place only at certain times of the year. Courtship describes the behaviour used by male animals to attract a female and mate with her. It informs a potential mate that the intention is breeding and not aggression. During courtship, males usually compete with each other to attract females, advertise that they are ready to mate, and encourage females to be sexually responsive. Females select males by the quality of their courtship display.

Male is aware that the female may lash out at him.

Male is attentive to the female.

Domestic cats
A female cat comes on heat, or is sexually responsive, about twice a year. She produces scents and calls loudly to attract males. Several males may compete for her by fighting. The successful male encourages the female by touching her and calling softly.

Female is sexually responsive and rolls.

Bird of paradise
Most birds have fixed courtship displays that ensure they attract a mate of the same species. Male birds often have brighter plumage than females, and this is especially true of the emperor bird of paradise. Males compete for females by quivering their long feathers and calling loudly.

Territorial behaviour

Many animals defend their territory to maintain access to food, water, shelter, and somewhere to reproduce. Territories can be large or small and held by one animal or by a group. Birdsong or the marking of territorial boundaries may deter rivals from entering a territory and avoid conflict and possible fatal injuries.

Cats
Most cats are solitary and maintain a territory on their own. Cheetahs patrol their territory and mark its boundaries by spraying urine on trees and other landmarks. The scent warns neighbouring cheetahs not to intrude.

Kittiwakes
Like many gull species, kittiwakes nest in colonies on narrow cliff ledges. Each pair of birds defends a small territory on the ledge, just large enough for the female to lay eggs and raise their young.

Aggression

Animals show aggression to other members of their species when competing for food, water, shelter, or mates. Some animals use horns, some use teeth or claws, and others kick. In many cases, animals signal their aggressive intent. This may defuse the situation and prevent injury.

Fighting bighorn sheep

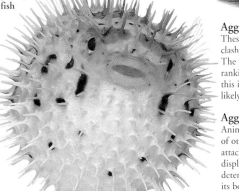

Inflated porcupine fish

Aggression within a species
These bighorn sheep use their horns to clash head-on in competition for mates. The winner of the fight gains higher social ranking and more females. Aggression like this is highly ritualized, and neither male is likely to be injured.

Aggression between species
Animals may be aggressive towards members of other species that are threatening or attacking them. Some animals use a threat display, often making themselves bigger to deter enemies. This porcupine fish inflates its body like a balloon and erects its spines.

Social behaviour

Social animals live in groups. Individuals co-operate to find food, defend themselves, and look after the young. Social groups range from shoals of fish, which are purely defensive, to societies of honeybees, where social organization affects all aspects of an individual's life.

Worker bee

Helping others
African wild dogs are social animals and often help each other. Male dogs will look after pups that are not their own, but were fathered by a brother or close relative. In this way they help pups to survive.

Living in large numbers
Many fish species swim close together in large numbers called shoals. A shoal moves and turns in a co-ordinated manner that mimics a single large living organism. Predators find it difficult to focus on one individual within the shoal.

Male bee, called a drone

Section of a bees' nest

Konrad Lorenz
Austrian zoologist Konrad Lorenz (1903-89) pioneered the study of animal behaviour. As part of his work on individual and group behaviour, Lorenz discovered imprinting. Lorenz shared a Nobel Prize in 1973 for his work.

Social insects
Within a colony of social insects, such as bees, there are groups that carry out certain tasks. In a bee colony a single queen lays eggs, while sterile female workers look after the young, collect food, and defend the colony. Male bees fertilize the queen.

FIND OUT MORE BIRDS FISH GENETICS INSECTS MAMMALS SONGBIRDS

ANIMALS

MORE THAN a million and a half species of animal have been identified, and there are many millions more yet to be discovered. Animals are living organisms found in nearly all of the Earth's habitats, including the depths of the oceans, the freezing Arctic, and even inside other animals and plants. The animal kingdom is divided into animals without backbones (invertebrates), such as snails and lobsters, and animals with backbones (vertebrates), such as frogs and monkeys. Invertebrates make up 97 per cent of all animal species.

Large eyes enable the leopard to see in dim light.

Body is covered with insulating fur and supported internally by a skeleton.

Long tail is a balancing aid.

Air is breathed in through nostrils.

Black leopard
The leopard is a mammal. Its well-defined head is equipped with sense organs, including eyes, nose, tongue, and whiskers. Sharp teeth in the mouth allow the leopard to kill prey and tear off flesh. Muscular legs enable it to walk, run, and pounce.

What is an animal?
Animals are made up of many cells. Most move actively, and those that are fixed in one place, or sedentary, move their body parts. Animals live by taking food into their bodies. They have sensors and nervous systems that enable them to detect what is happening around them and respond appropriately.

Giant land flatworm

Animal classification
Animals are classified into groups according to their similarities and whether they have common ancestors. There are 35 major groups called phyla (singular phylum). Each phylum is divided into sub-groups. The smallest of these is the species, which contains animals of just one type.

Sponge processed for human use *Sea anemones*

Sponges
The simplest animals are sponges (phylum Porifera). There are about 5,000 species, most of which live in the sea attached to rocks and other objects. Water is drawn in through holes, or pores, in the sponge's body wall, and bits of food are filtered out and eaten by the sponge's cells.

Cnidarians
There are more than 9,000 species of cnidarians (phylum Cnidaria), most of which are found in the sea. They include jellyfish, sea anemones, hydras, and corals. Cnidarians catch food using tentacles armed with stinging threads, called nematocysts.

Flatworms
These worms (phylum Platyhelminthes) have a flattened body with one opening, the mouth, on the underside. There are about 18,500 species including those, such as tapeworms, that are parasites of humans and other animals.

Nematodes
Roundworms, or nematodes (phylum Nematoda), have a thin, cylindrical body that is pointed at both ends. Free-living nematodes are found in many habitats and occur in very large numbers in soil. Many nematodes are parasites of plants and animals.

Threadworm

Annelids
Animals in the phylum Annelida include earthworms, marine bristleworms such as ragworms, and leeches. There are about 12,000 species, each of which has a body made up of segments with a mouth at one end and an anus at the other.

King ragworm

Stalked eye *Coiled shell protects the soft body.*

Snail emerging from its shell.

Molluscs
Molluscs (phylum Mollusca) form a highly diverse group of about 50,000 species. These include snails and slugs, mussels and clams, and squids and octopuses. They are soft-bodied animals that may be protected by a shell. Most live in water, but some, such as snails, are found on land.

Snail moves on a muscular foot. *Sensory tentacle* *Head and foot fully extended*

Echinoderms
All echinoderms (phylum Echinodermata) live in the sea. The 6,500 or so species include sea urchins and starfish. Most have five parts radiating from a central point, hard plates under the skin, and many tube-feet.

Cushion star *Bloody Henry starfish* *Cushion star*

Arthropods have hard, jointed external skeletons.

Arthropods
With at least one million known species, Arthropods (phylum Arthropoda) are the largest group of animals. They include insects, crustaceans (such as crabs), arachnids (such as spiders), and centipedes.

Sharp teeth to grasp food

Chordates
There are about 48,000 species of chordate (phylum Chordata). Most are vertebrates, such as fish, amphibians, reptiles, birds, and mammals. Vertebrates are the most advanced animals.

Tail used for movement or balance is typical of many vertebrates.

Caiman *Tarantula*

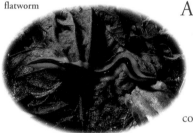

A

Animal skeletons

The skeleton is a supportive framework that maintains the shape of an animal and enables it to move. Most skeletons are hard structures, either inside or outside the animal's body, to which muscles are attached. The skeleton may also protect internal organs and, in the case of an insect's external skeleton, prevent the animal from drying out.

Limbs and head attached to backbone

Crab's exoskeleton

Salamander's endoskeleton

Internal skeletons
A skeleton found inside the body is called an endoskeleton. Most vertebrates have a skeleton made of cartilage and bone. Joints between the bones allow the animal to move. The endoskeleton grows with the rest of the body.

External skeletons
A hard outer skeleton that covers all or part of the body is called an exoskeleton. An insect's outer cuticle and a snail's shell are examples of an exoskeleton. An insect's exoskeleton does not grow and must be shed, or moulted, periodically to allow the animal to grow.

Earthworm

Hydrostatic skeleton
The hydrostatic skeleton is an internal skeleton found in soft-bodied animals such as earthworms. It consists of a fluid-filled core surrounded by muscles, and maintains the shape of the worm.

Worm gets longer when it contracts its muscles.

Movement of an eel through water

Eel moves by throwing its body into curves that push against the water.

Animal movement

The ability to move is characteristic of animals, which move to find food, escape from predators, and find a mate. The way in which an animal moves depends on its complexity, lifestyle, and where it lives. The wide range of movement includes swimming through water, walking and creeping on land, and flying or gliding in air.

Wings sweep downward to produce forward thrust.

Movement in air
Insects, birds, and bats are capable of powered flight using wings. Birds have lightweight, streamlined bodies. They use energy to flap their wings, which pushes them forward. As air passes over the wings it creates the lift that keeps the bird in the air.

Young chaffinch in flight

Moving in water
Many aquatic animals are adapted for movement in water by having streamlined bodies. Most fish move by pushing their tail fin from side to side. This pushes the water backward and sideways, and propels the fish forward. Whales move in a similar way, except that the tail moves up and down.

Asian elephant

Feet expand under the elephant's weight as they are put down.

Movement on land
Animals move on land in a variety of ways. Many have limbs that raise the body off the ground, support it, and enable the animal to walk, run, or hop. The animals move forward by pushing the ends of their legs, or feet, backward against the ground.

Animal senses

The main senses are vision, hearing, taste, smell, and touch. Animals use their senses to find out what is going on around them. A stimulus from outside, such as a sound, is detected by a sense organ, such as the ear. Nerve impulses from sense organs are interpreted by the animal's brain which "decides" how to respond.

Dragonfly eyes

Eyes
Eyes contain sensors that are sensitive to light. When stimulated they send nerve impulses to the brain, which enable it to build up a picture. Insects have compound eyes made up of many separate units, or ommatidia.

Feeding

All animals feed by taking in food. They use a range of feeding strategies and can be grouped accordingly. Some animals kill and eat others, some graze or browse on plants, others filter food particles from water. After feeding, or ingestion, food is digested so that it can be used by the body.

Mormon caterpillar consuming a leaf

Herbivores
Animals that feed solely on plants are called herbivores. Many use specialized mouthparts, such as grinding teeth, to break up tough plant tissues. Plant material is not a rich food source, and most herbivores eat a lot to obtain the necessary nutrients.

Longhorn beetle

Antennae
These are found on the head of arthropods such as insects. They are used to detect odours and may detect chemicals called pheromones released by insects to communicate with each other. Antennae also detect vibrations and movements in the air or in water.

External ear flaps channel sounds into the ear.

Ears
Some animals can detect sounds with ears. The ear converts sounds into nerve impulses that can be interpreted by the animal's brain. Animals use sounds to communicate with each other and to detect approaching predators or prey.

Domestic Basenji dog

Giant clam

Filter feeders
These are animals that feed by sieving food particles from water that flows into their body. Many are sedentary and draw in a current of water. Some whales are filter feeders that eat small animals called krill.

Carnivores
These types of feeders are adapted to detect prey animals, to catch and kill them, and to cut them up to eat them. They include cats, eagles, and some insects. Dragonfly larvae live in water and they can catch small fish to eat.
Dragonfly larva with stickleback

FIND OUT MORE   AMPHIBIANS   ANIMAL BEHAVIOUR   BIRDS   FISH   FLIGHT, ANIMAL   INSECTS   MAMMALS   REPTILES   SNAILS AND OTHER MOLLUSCS

ANTARCTICA

WITH THE SOUTH POLE at its heart, Antarctica is the world's windiest, coldest, and most southerly continent. The last region on Earth to be explored, this huge landmass is not divided into countries, but seven countries claimed territories there. In 1959, however, the Antarctic Treaty suspended those claims and stated that the continent is to be used for peaceful purposes only. Antarctica's sole inhabitants are visiting scientists, working in research stations.

Physical features

Antarctica is almost entirely covered by a vast sheet of ice, in places 4.8 km (3 miles) deep. It contains 90 per cent of the Earth's ice, and 80 per cent of the world's fresh water. The vast Ronne and Ross ice shelves are formed where the ice sheet extends over the ocean.

Icebergs

Currents beneath Antarctica's vast ice shelves cause giant slabs of ice to break away, the largest of which may be 200 km (124 miles) long. As these enormous icebergs drift north they slowly break up and melt. Only the top third of an iceberg shows above the water.

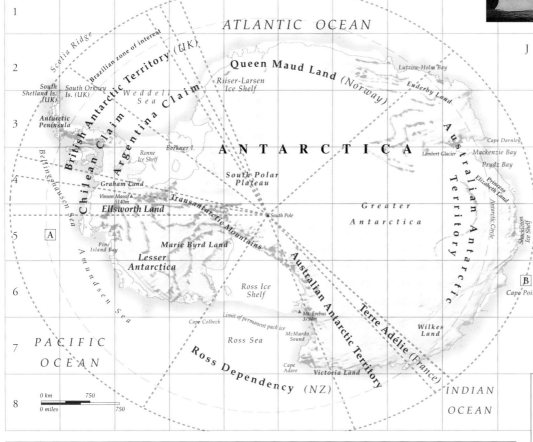

Mount Erebus

Antarctica has volcanic areas. An active volcano, Mount Erebus, lies on Ross Island on the edge of the Ross Ice Shelf. It forms part of the Transantarctic mountain chain that includes peaks up to 4,570 m (15,000 ft) high.

Tourism

Cruise ships bring around 9,000 people each year to see Antarctica's coastline and wildlife. A hotel now exists on King George Island. Tourists who venture on to the ice must wear insulated clothing and goggles to protect their eyes from the glare.

Tourists shelter in a whale skull

Cross-section through Antarctica

The Transantarctic mountains divide the continent of Antarctica into Greater and Lesser Antarctica. Although the land itself is low, the depth of the ice on top of it makes Antarctica the highest continent, with an average height of 2,100 m (6,900 ft). The ice-cap was formed by the build up of snow over the last 100,000 years and contains 90 per cent of the world's ice.

West Antarctic Ice Sheet (Lesser Antarctica) *Ross Ice Shelf* *Transantarctic Mountains* *East Antarctic Ice Sheet (Greater Antarctica)*

A — Approximately 6,000 km (3,728 miles) from A to B — B

FIND OUT MORE | ATLANTIC OCEAN | CLIMATE | GLACIATION | INDIAN OCEAN | PACIFIC OCEAN | POLAR EXPLORATION | POLAR WILDLIFE | POLLUTION | VOLCANOES

ANTEATERS, SLOTHS AND ARMADILLOS

A BIZARRE GROUP of animals make up the order of mammals known as the edentates. They include the anteaters, armadillos, and sloths, all of which, except the nine-banded armadillo, live in the tropical regions of South and Central America. The name "edentate" means "without teeth", but it is a misleading term, as only the anteaters are toothless. In fact, some armadillos have more teeth than any other land mammal.

Young
A female anteater gives birth to a single young. The young anteater travels on its mother's back for the first year of its life, by which time it is almost half the size of its mother.

Anteater
There are four species of anteater. The giant anteater lives in grasslands; the other three species live in forests and have prehensile (grasping) tails with which they hang from trees. Anteaters have long snouts and tongues to enable them to collect the termites and ants on which they feed. They locate their prey with their acute sense of smell. Their foreclaws are so large that they need to walk on their knuckles. The claws are used to break open termite nests and for defence. If threatened, they rear up on their hind legs and try to rip their opponent with their claws.

Giant anteater breaking into a termite mound.

Long bushy tail

Giant anteater

Tongue
Anteaters have long sticky tongues that can be pushed deep into termite nests. The tongue is covered in little spines that point backwards, making it very difficult for ants and termites to escape.

Curved spines on tongue

Armadillo
Of the 21 species of armadillo, the largest is the giant armadillo, which is 91.5 cm (3 ft) in length. It has up to 100 peg-like teeth – twice as many as most mammals – which are shed when the animal reaches adulthood. The smallest species, the fairy armadillo, is less than 15 cm (6 in) long. Armadillos give birth to up to four young. The nine-banded armadillo, from North America, gives birth to quadruplets of the same sex.

Claws
Armadillos have large curved claws. They use them to dig into the ground to make burrows, to escape predators, and to find food. The giant armadillo's middle claw is the largest claw in the animal kingdom, measuring 18 cm (7 in) around the curve.

Nine-banded armadillo

Bony plates

Large claws

Hairy stomach

Nine-banded armadillo

Body armour
Armadillos are encased in "body armour" formed by separate plates made of bone. Soft skin links the plates together, giving them flexibility. In most species the plates cover only the upper part of the body. If threatened, some species, such as the three-banded armadillo, roll into a ball, while others make for their burrow or dig themselves into the ground.

Sloth
Adapted to living upside down, sloths hang by their claws from the branches of trees. They can rotate their heads through a 270° angle, allowing them to keep their head upright while their body remains inverted. They eat, mate, give birth, and spend their entire life-cycle upside down. Sloth's hair lies in the opposite direction from other animals', to allow rain to run off. Only when asleep do they adopt a more normal position, by squatting in the fork of a tree. There are seven species of sloth; all are herbivorous.

Movement
Sloths are very slow movers. They rarely descend to the ground as they can only just stand, but cannot walk. They drag themselves along with their claws. In water though, they are good swimmers.

Sloth swimming

Female three-toed sloth with baby

Green algae cover the sloth's coat.

Camouflage
Due to the high humidity levels in the rainforest, infestations of green algae grow within a sloth's fur and cover its coat. This acts as a camouflage and makes the sloth less conspicuous. As the seasons change, the algae change colour to match the colour of the trees.

Pangolin
There are seven species of pangolin, or scaly anteater. They have much in common with the edentates, but they belong to a different order called the Pholidota. They are covered with scales attached to the skin. Some species have a long, prehensile tail that is used to grasp branches and also to lash out at predators. They feed on termites, ants, and larvae which they catch with their long tongues.

Malayan pangolin

GIANT ANTEATER

SCIENTIFIC NAME	*Myrmecophaga tridactyla*
ORDER	Edentata
FAMILY	Myrmecophagidae
DISTRIBUTION	South America
HABITAT	Grasslands and savannahs
DIET	Termites, ants, and larvae
SIZE	Length, including tail: 1.83 m (6 ft)
LIFESPAN	25 years (in captivity)

FIND OUT MORE

ASIAN WILDLIFE · CAMOUFLAGE AND COLOUR · CONSERVATION · GRASSLAND WILDLIFE · MAMMALS · RAINFOREST WILDLIFE · SOUTH AMERICAN WILDLIFE

ANTS AND TERMITES

A

FOR EVERY HUMAN, there are 1,000,000 ants. Ants and termites are social insects that live in large colonies and have developed complex systems of communication. Ants are found worldwide, but, like termites, most of the 9,500 species of ant live in the tropics. There are more than 2,400 types of termite; many are blind, spending their lives inside nests, never seeing the light of day.

Ants

Ants have two pairs of compound eyes, three single eyes, or ocelli, two antennae, and three pairs of legs. Only queens and males have wings. A narrow waist connects the thorax and abdomen. Ants undergo complete metamorphosis, from an egg to larval and pupal stages, before emerging as adults. They live in huge groups and each ant has a particular role. The queen runs the nest and mates with male ants. Workers are female and gather food and nurse the eggs, larvae, and pupae. Soldier ants, also female, guard the nest.

Eyes · *Pheromones are released from the abdomen.* · *Thorax* · *Legs are attached to the thorax.* · **Wood ants**

Bull ant

Antennae are used to pick up the scent of pheromones. · *Eyes* · *Spiked jaws used to attack prey and predators.*

Communication
Ants lay trails of pheromones – chemicals that smell – so that other ants can follow them by using their sensitive antennae to pick up the smell. This helps foraging teams home in on food.

Defence
If a nest is attacked, the ants release pheromones to warn each other. Most run for cover, but soldier ants get aggressive and defend the colony. They attack enemies with their large jaws, or sting them and inject formic acid, which causes extreme pain. Some ants even explode to shower an attacker in venom.

Ant nest
Most ants live in nests or colonies, usually underground. However, weaver ants build nests out of leaves in trees, and army ants build "live nests" of worker ants. Normally, there is one queen in a nest, but there are sometimes several. Nests of Australian bull ants contain up to 600 ants, while some wood ants' nests can house more than 300 million.

"Live nest" made by army ants

Feeding
Many ants are omnivores and eat seeds, nectar, and invertebrates. Army and driver ants are more carnivorous, and kill and eat prey such as worms, spiders, and even some lizards. Leaf-cutting ants are one of a few species of herbivorous ants. They feed on a type of fungus, which grows on the chewed-up remains of leaves and flowers that the ants take back to their nests.

Ants carrying pieces of leaves back to their nest.

Leaf-cutting ants

Termites

Although often called white ants, termites belong to a totally different order, the Isoptera. Like ants, termites live in large colonies. Unlike ants, termites do not have waists, and the male, called a king, does not die after mating, but lives with the queen. They do not go through complete metamorphosis, but grow up gradually through several nymphal stages.

Soldiers
Like ants, termites have soldiers. Termites cannot sting, but defend themselves in other ways. Some soldiers have large jaws that can cut through flesh; others squirt a poisonous sticky liquid from a special nozzle on their heads. Some nests have no soldiers – the termites defend themselves by vibrating their bodies against the side of their nest, making the sound of a hissing snake.

Pincers

Queen and king
A queen termite can reach more than 15 cm (6 in) in length. Her ovaries make her so large. She can lay up to 30,000 eggs a day. The king remains by the queen's side and mates with her several times to fertilize all the eggs.

Queen

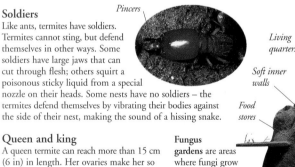

Fungus
gardens are areas where fungi grow on termites' faeces and break down the cellulose within them. The termites feed on the products released and the fungi itself.

"Chimneys" allow warm air to rise and escape.
Solid outer walls are up to 50 cm (20 in) thick.
Living quarters
Soft inner walls
Food stores
Air channel
Ground level
Nurseries
Royal chamber
Thick pillar supports nest.
Termites spread water on walls to cool the nest.

Termite mounds
Each species of termite has its own type of nest. Some build towers more than 6 m (20 ft) tall, which help maintain the correct temperature and humidity of the nest at the base. Others build mushroom-shaped mounds – the domed top deflects the rain away from the nest below and has given these insects their name of umbrella termites. Many termites do not build nests above ground, but live below the soil or inside logs. Termites that live in trees build their nests on branches.

Workers
Worker termites build the nest, collect food, and feed the soldiers, king, and queen. The nest is made from saliva, soil, and their own faeces. Most workers feed on wood and have microscopic organisms in their guts to break down the wood into a more easily digested form.

WOOD ANT	
SCIENTIFIC NAME	*Formica rufa*
ORDER	Hymenoptera
FAMILY	Formicidae
DISTRIBUTION	Europe
HABITAT	Woods and forests
DIET	Omnivorous, feeding on seeds and invertebrates
SIZE	Workers 6–8 mm (0.24–0.31 in) in length; queen 10–13 mm (0.4–0.5 in) in length
LIFESPAN	Workers live for 3–4 months; the queen lives for about 15 years

FIND OUT MORE · ANIMAL BEHAVIOUR · ARTHROPODS · INSECTS · MONGOOSES AND CIVETS · MUSHROOMS AND OTHER FUNGI · NESTS AND BURROWS · WOODLAND WILDLIFE

ARCHAEOLOGY

HUMANKIND HAS ALWAYS been fascinated by the question of who we are, where we came from, and how we used to live. Archaeology is the study of our past, from early prehistory onward, using the material remains of our ancestors and the possessions they left behind. Over thousands of years, evidence of human activity, such as camp fires, rubbish tips, and dwellings, become buried. Archaeological teams discover these sites and uncover this evidence by careful excavation. The material is then conserved and studied in order to help the archaeologist piece together a picture of how people lived and died in the past.

Discovery

Iron Age fort, England

Archaeological sites are found during building work, through reading historical documents, geophysical surveys (the study of the soil's structure), and field walking (recording above-ground objects).

Aerial photography
Horizontal and vertical lines seen from the air often show medieval strip fields, ancient roads, walls, and ditches. Aerial photography done when the sun is low shows varying surface levels, moisture levels, and vegetation most clearly.

Excavation

Archaeological sites are excavated by layers. Workers remove the top, most recent layer and work down, uncovering older, deeper levels. The study of these layers and the items they contain is called stratigraphy.

Stratigraphy
By revealing features such as ditches, post holes, and floors, stratigraphy gives information about the history of a site, and the people who lived there. In urban areas, such as London, surface levels rise as debris is shovelled in to level the ground before rebuilding. Because it shows a chronological sequence, stratigraphy was used to date sites before radiocarbon dating was invented.

17th-century floor · *19th-century drain* · *16th-century chalk floor*

Cross section through a dig, City of London

Brick-lined well, c.1800 · *14th-century chalk-lined cesspit* · *Roman tiled floor*

Tools

Pickaxe

Trowel · *Measuring tape*

Archaeologists use shovels and handpicks to remove the topsoil. Then smaller hand tools are used, such as dental picks, teaspoons, and trowels, to excavate delicate objects.

Finds
Archaeologists usually draw or photograph the artefacts (objects) to make a visual record. They carefully measure and record the shapes, colours, decorations, and ages of any artefacts or features. This helps archaeologists link and relate different objects and sites.

Investigation

Buried objects are fragile, and decay quickly after excavation. To stabilize them, they are cleaned and conserved. After conservation, an object can be studied. The material of which it is made, its function, and its date are recorded. It may then be photographed and displayed in a museum.

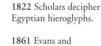

Salt water has caused corrosion

Pewter Jug

A cradle hoisted the ship from the seabed.

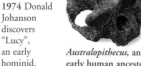

Underwater archaeology
Sites beneath the sea or in lakes are more difficult to excavate than those on land because shifting silt or sand causes poor visibility. However, marine sites often preserve materials, such as the wood of the 16th-century ship, the *Mary Rose*, which would usually be lost on dry land. Conservation may involve treatment with water, sealing with chemicals, or careful drying.

To conserve the wood, chilled water is sprayed on the ship 20 hours a day.

The *Mary Rose* in dry dock

Timeline

1748 Pompeii discovered.

1799 An officer in Napoleon's army discovers the Rosetta Stone, which features 6th-century BC hieroglyphs.

1812 Abu Simbel discovered.

1822 Scholars decipher Egyptian hieroglyphs.

1861 Evans and Prestwich confirm the antiquity of humans, and humans' association with extinct animals.

1891 *Homo erectus* material found.

1922 Howard Carter discovers the tomb of Tutankhamun.

1931 Louis Leakey begins excavations at Olduvai Gorge.

1940 Archaeologists discover prehistoric Lascaux cave paintings.

1949 Radiocarbon dating is developed.

1974 Donald Johanson discovers "Lucy", an early hominid.

Australopithecus, an early human ancestor

Mortimer Wheeler

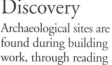

The greatest field archaeologist of the day, Wheeler (1890–1976) set up the Institute of Archaeology, London. He developed new excavation methods, and made archaeology popular through TV. In 1944, he became Director-General of Archaeology in India, and investigated the Indus Valley Civilization.

FIND OUT MORE · ASIA, HISTORY OF · BRONZE AGE · EUROPE, HISTORY OF · HUMAN EVOLUTION · PREHISTORIC PEOPLE · STONE AGE

Archaeological finds from the *Mary Rose*

Weapons

Swivel guns

Hailshot pieces

Closed hand

Lint held at this end

Wrought-iron breech chambers

Longbows made of yew

Linstock handle

Demi cannon, a cast bronze muzzle loader

Culverin, a cast bronze muzzle loader

Stone, iron, and lead shot, used for cannon

Wooden linstocks held the slow match (lint), which the crew used to light gunpowder in cannon.

Breech loader gun, made of wrought iron

Shipboard equipment

Wooden razor handles

Apothecary's balance

Deadeye

Personal sundial

Ceramic medicine jar

An angel, a 1545 gold coin

Bronze cooking pot, used for communal meals

Wooden tankard

Pewter spoon and plates were used at the captain's dinner table.

Clothing and personal

Manicure set, made of bone

Wooden comb

Inkpot, made of horn

Leather jerkin

Backgammon set

Yew and spruce inlay

Leather flask for storing wine or water

Leather book cover

A

ARCHITECTURE

FROM A TOWERING SKYSCRAPER to a functional factory, architecture is the art of planning a building. The word also refers to the different building styles seen throughout history. Looking at changes in architecture tells us about earlier societies: the materials that were available to their builders, the skills mastered by their engineers, and the social ideals that they wished to express in their public buildings.

Architectural features

The main structural and functional features of a building are the roof, arches and walls, doors, and windows. The architect combines the practical knowledge of how to construct these with a sense of how to combine shape, space, and light to suit the function of the building itself.

Groin

Vault

Groin vault, where two barrel vaults intersect

Main arch

Barrel vault

Round arch

Arch and vault
An arch is a curved or pointed structure that bridges a gap; it must carry the weight of the wall, floor, or roof above, and its structure allows it to support greater weight than a flat slab can. A vault is simply an arched ceiling.

Classical Europe

Classical architecture is that of the ancient Greeks and Romans. Both built by laying stones on top of each other, or by resting beams on columns. The Romans also developed the arch, vault, dome, and the use of concrete to develop curved spaces.

Use of concrete
Cheap and durable, this material allowed Roman architects to cover vast curved spaces, which were impossible to construct before.

Opening

Dome, 43 m (142 ft) across

Walls 6 m (21 ft) thick

Outer wall faced with brick

Corinthian column

Entrance porch, or portico

The Pantheon, Rome, Italy, completed c. AD 128

Ornament
Early in the 20th century, many Western architects rejected all forms of building ornament. This is rare: most buildings from other periods and cultures use it extensively, and even a simple building will usually have some decoration to reflect the taste of its owner. The ancient Greeks, for instance, carved the tops, or capitals, of columns to dignify their most prestigious buildings. The distinct decorations were based on styles called orders.

Doric order

Ionic order

Corinthian order

A

Cross and orb

Dome metalling, Church of the Sorbonne, Paris, France, 17th century

Lantern (turret with windows) provides light

Round-arched window

Dome on a circular base

Eaves

Pitched roof, supporting frame

Main rafter (inclined beam)

Horizontal beams add strength to structure.

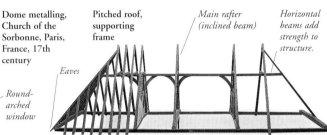

Dome
Domes – curved, solid roofs – were first built on palaces and religious buildings as striking symbols of the building's status. They are often difficult to build, and have been constructed in various shapes: the Dome of the Rock in Jerusalem is hemispherical; the "onion"-shaped dome is a popular feature of many Russian and Bavarian buildings.

Roof
All roofs are designed for the practical purpose of providing protection from the weather. The design and covering used will reflect the local climate: for instance, in a wet country a sloping (pitched) roof will let rain run off. Roofs can also be ingenious and beautiful, such as when crowning an ornate castle.

Brunelleschi
Italian architect Filippo Brunelleschi (1377–1446) returned to the use of Classical features, rejecting the Gothic style. Architects all across Europe followed his example.

Symbolism
The Pantheon is a temple built to all the Roman gods. Light comes through an opening in its vast dome and moves around the interior, lighting the curved walls. It is as if even the Universe turns around the centre of the building, symbolizing the power of the Roman deities.

Gothic

This distinctive, ornate European style emerged in the 12th century, and was used mainly in cathedrals and churches. Features include pointed arches and windows, and elaborate stone tracery used to divide the openings in window arches.

Eight-sided spire, built using scaffolding and wooden cranes

Turret-like pinnacle

Building innovations
The pointed arch and flying buttress were innovations that allowed Gothic churches to soar higher than had been possible before. Pointed arches can support heavier, taller structures than round arches. The flying buttress is a stone rib which extends down and away from the walls, transferring weight to the ground, and giving extra support to a roof or walls.

Pointed arch

Flying buttress

Pointed arch filled with tracery

Pitched roof

Buttress

Old St. Paul's Cathedral, London, England, 1087–1666

A

Southeast Asia and the Middle East

The traditional architectural styles of Asia and the Middle East remained the same for centuries. Both were heavily influenced by religious belief: Buddhism and Hinduism in southern Asia, and Islam in the Middle East. The style of buildings was determined by climate, and the materials available to local builders. As early as the 7th century, wooden temples and monasteries were being built in China and Japan.

Pagoda in Burmese style, 9th–10th century

Gilded crown

Minaret

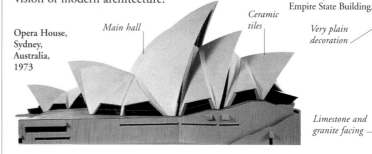
Islamic decoration favours geometric patterns and calligraphy.

South and East Asia
Many of the distinctive features of this area's architecture originated in Buddhist India. An example is the multi-storeyed pagoda, a temple which seems to stretch towards Heaven. It was developed initially in Japan and China but was based on the spires found on early Indian temples. An important feature of many traditional Asian buildings is their imaginative roof forms.

Islamic architecture
The most important buildings in Islamic countries are usually mosques and tombs. The mosque is the centre of a Muslim community, and provides space for group worship. It contains a prayer hall, often with a domed roof, and may also have a courtyard. A minaret, from which the faithful are called to prayer, is a typical feature.

Early American civilizations

The Aztecs, who ruled in what is now Mexico from the 14th to 16th centuries, built stone pyramids to their gods. The remains of five separate temples have been found at Tenochtitlan, built one on top of the other as new rulers erected bigger temples on the same site.

Shrine to Aztec god

Stone carving of snake's head

Outer stone covering

Remains of different temples

Baroque and Neoclassical

The Baroque style emerged in early 17th-century Europe. It introduced buildings with ornate decoration, complex shapes, and dramatic lighting. It was followed by the Neoclassical style, which revived the more restrained Classical traditions. This was partly as a reaction to Baroque excess.

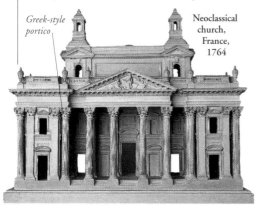

Greek-style portico

Neoclassical church, France, 1764

The 19th and 20th centuries

The development of new, very strong materials made it possible to construct buildings which were often highly original in style and owed little to the past. Helped by better technology, architects turned to glass, steel, and concrete to express their vision of modern architecture.

Opera House, Sydney, Australia, 1973

Main hall

Ceramic tiles

Interlocked vaults
The dramatic profile of the Opera House dominates Sydney Harbour. The building's roof of interlocked vaults, made from reinforced concrete covered with gleaming tiles, resembles a ship in sail.

Skyscrapers
The invention of the lift during the 19th century made it practical to build skyscrapers, and the first appeared in Chicago, USA, in the 1880s. Today, most are constructed for large businesses: they convey perfectly an image of wealth, size, and strength.

Proposed design

Architects
An architect designs a building and oversees its construction. Successful architects become very well-known. Until recently, architects drew large numbers of plans to instruct builders and engineers. Much of this work is now carried out on computer.

Steel
Following the arrival of reinforced steel, very tall structures could be built for the first time. An internal steel skeleton supports the weight of a skyscraper, such as the 102 storeys of the Empire State Building.

Empire State Building, New York, USA, 1931

Very plain decoration

Limestone and granite facing

Le Corbusier
Le Corbusier was the name used by the Swiss-French Charles Édouard Jeanneret (1887–1965), the most influential 20th-century architect. Le Corbusier promoted the use of new materials and construction techniques. His imaginative buildings favoured plain, often severe, geometric forms.

Timeline

2650 BC The Step Pyramid in Egypt is designed.

c.300 BC Buddhist temple mounds appear in India.

AD 82 Colosseum built in Rome. Dozens of stone arches support the walls of this stone arena.

690–850 Early Islamic buildings are designed around courtyards.

1100–1500 Gothic churches built in Europe.

c.1420 Renaissance begins in Italy; architects return to the elegant, ordered values of Classical builders.

19th century Industrial Revolution: mass-produced materials transform construction.

1920s International Modernism begins, typified by glass-and-steel towers and flat-roofed, white houses.

1970s Postmodernism develops. It refers to past styles, in a humorous way. Strong colours are popular.

1990s Eco-friendly architecture reflects environmental concerns about energy-saving and recycling.

FIND OUT MORE

BUILDING AND CONSTRUCTION   CHURCHES AND CATHEDRALS   CITIES   MOSQUES

Architecture

Gothic, Renaissance, and Baroque

Magnificent Gothic cathedral

Two lions flank the entrance.

Notre Dame, Paris, France: built from 1163 to 1250.

Carved stone lantern

Palacio de las Cadenas, Ubeda, Spain: built during the mid-16th century. The Classical facade shows the elegance of Renaissance buildings.

St. Paul's Cathedral, London, Britain: built in the Baroque style.

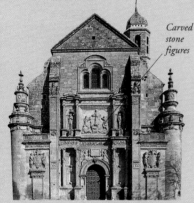

Carved stone figures

Capilla del Salvador, Ubeda, Spain: one of Spain's finest Renaissance churches, it was designed by three 16th-century architects.

Ribbed dome designed by Michelangelo

Facade by Carlo Maderno (c.1556–1629)

St. Peter's, Rome, Italy, took over a century to build (1506–1614). It involved all the great architects of the Roman Renaissance and Baroque, including Michelangelo Buonarroti (1475–1564).

135 spires crown the roof.

Milan Cathedral, Italy, is one of the largest Gothic churches in the world. Building began in the 14th century, but was not completed for 500 years.

Modern architecture

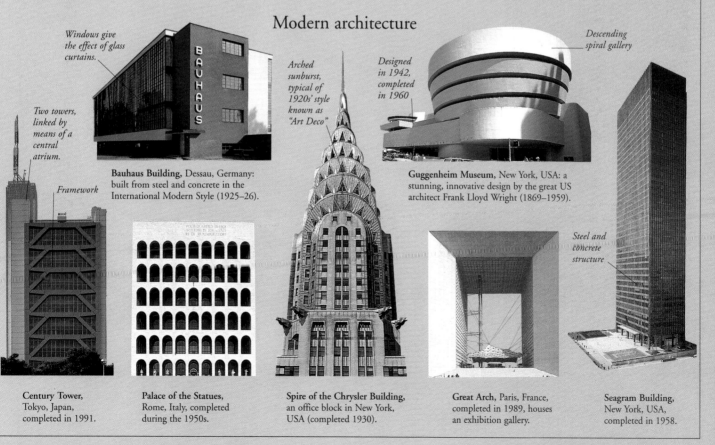

Windows give the effect of glass curtains.

Two towers, linked by means of a central atrium.

Framework

Century Tower, Tokyo, Japan, completed in 1991.

Arched sunburst, typical of 1920s' style known as "Art Deco"

Bauhaus Building, Dessau, Germany: built from steel and concrete in the International Modern Style (1925–26).

Palace of the Statues, Rome, Italy, completed during the 1950s.

Spire of the Chrysler Building, an office block in New York, USA (completed 1930).

Designed in 1942, completed in 1960

Descending spiral gallery

Guggenheim Museum, New York, USA: a stunning, innovative design by the great US architect Frank Lloyd Wright (1869–1959).

Great Arch, Paris, France, completed in 1989, houses an exhibition gallery.

Steel and concrete structure

Seagram Building, New York, USA, completed in 1958.

ARCTIC OCEAN

ONE OF THE COLDEST places on Earth, the Arctic Ocean is surrounded by the northern parts of Europe, Asia, North America, and Greenland. These icy lands are rich in minerals and wildlife, but are home to few people. In summer, when temperatures reach 0°C (32°F), warm currents from the Pacific and Atlantic melt some of the ice. With the help of icebreakers to clear their path, ships are able to sail along the coasts of Asia and North America.

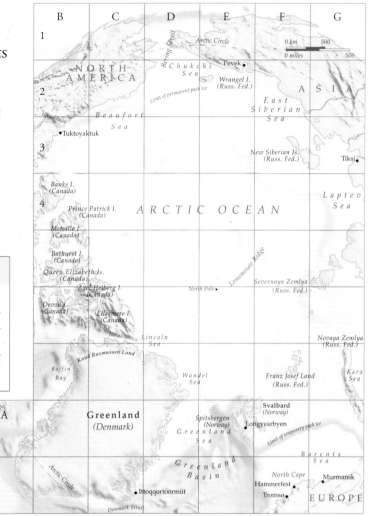

Physical features

The Arctic is the smallest and shallowest of the world's oceans. Most of its surface is covered by a frozen mass of floating ice about 2 m (6 ft) thick. The North Pole lies in the centre of the Arctic Ocean on drifting pack ice.

ARCTIC OCEAN FACTS

AREA 14,089,600 sq km (5,440,000 sq miles)

AVERAGE DEPTH 1,330 m (4,360 ft)

AVERAGE ICE THICKNESS 1.5–3 m (4.9–9.8 ft)

LOWEST TEMPERATURE -70°C (-94°F) on northeast tip of Greenland

Icebergs
Giant icebergs break off glaciers in Greenland and drift south into the North Atlantic Ocean. They rise up to 120 m (400 ft) above sea-level. As only a fraction of an iceberg shows above water, they are a shipping hazard.

Northern lights
On dark nights, spectacular coloured lights, or Aurora, can be seen in the sky. Caused by electricity in the upper atmosphere, they are brightest in mid winter when the sun never rises and invisible in summer due to 24-hour sun.

Arctic peoples
About 800,000 indigenous people live in the Arctic. The Yu'pik of Alaska are part of the Eskimo group that includes Inuit in Canada and Greenland and Yuit in Siberia. Many have given up nomadic life and now live in villages. The Arctic is the workplace of about 2,000,000 engineers and traders from the south.

Yu'pik family from Alaska

Greenland
Although Greenland is the world's largest island, its permanent ice cover means few people live there. The most populated area is the southwest coast, where the climate is less extreme than the bleak centre. The island is a self-governing territory of Denmark.

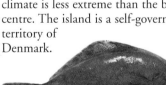

Halibut

Haddock

Cod

GREENLAND FACTS

CAPITAL CITY Nuuk (Godthaab)

AREA 2,175,600 sq km (840,000 sq miles)

POPULATION 56,569

MAIN LANGUAGES Danish, Greenlandic

MAJOR RELIGION Christian

CURRENCY Danish krone

Fishing
Cod, haddock, halibut, and shrimp fishing are the mainstay of Greenland's economy. Fish-processing factories freeze and can the fish for export to Europe and the USA. Much of the cod is made into fish fingers.

FIND OUT MORE ATMOSPHERE CLIMATE FISHING INDUSTRY GLACIATION NATIVE AMERICANS OCEANS AND SEAS POLAR EXPLORATION POLAR WILDLIFE TUNDRA